CLEVER Lili

27

STUDY GUIDE

Conflict and Tension between East and West, 1945–1972

AQA - GCSE

app
available

Published by Clever Lili Limited.

contact@cleverlili.com

First published 2020

ISBN 978-1-913887-26-1

Cover by: Twindesigner on Adobe Stock

Icons by: flaticon and freepik

Contributors: Lynn Harkin, James George, Alex Price

Edited by Paul Connolly and Rebecca Parsley

Design by Evgeni Veskov and Will Fox

DISCOVER MORE OF OUR GCSE HISTORY STUDY GUIDES

GCSEHistory.com and Clever Lili

AQA - GCSE

STUDY GUIDE

Britain: Health and the People, c1000 to the Present Day

GCSEHistory.com

25

AQA - GCSE

STUDY GUIDE

Elizabethan England, c1568-1603

GCSEHistory.com

26

AQA - GCSE

STUDY GUIDE

Germany, 1890-1945: Democracy and Dictatorship

GCSEHistory.com

28

AQA - GCSE

STUDY GUIDE

America, 1920-1973: Opportunity and Inequality

GCSEHistory.com

29

AQA - GCSE

STUDY GUIDE

Britain: Power and the People, c1170 to the Present Day

GCSEHistory.com

30

AQA - GCSE

STUDY GUIDE

Norman England, c1066 -c1100

GCSEHistory.com

35

AQA - GCSE

STUDY GUIDE

Conflict and Tension: The First World War, 1894-1918

GCSEHistory.com

36

AQA - GCSE

STUDY GUIDE

Russia, 1894-1945: Tsardom and Communism

GCSEHistory.com

43

AQA - GCSE

STUDY GUIDE

America, 1840-1895: Expansion and Consolidation

GCSEHistory.com

38

AQA - GCSE

STUDY GUIDE

Conflict and Tension: The Inter-War Years, 1918-1939

GCSEHistory.com

41

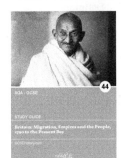

AQA - GCSE

STUDY GUIDE

Britain: Migration, Empires and the People, c790 to the Present Day

GCSEHistory.com

44

AQA - GCSE

STUDY GUIDE

Conflict and Tension in Asia, 1950-1975

GCSEHistory.com

45

THE GUIDES ARE EVEN BETTER WITH OUR GCSE/IGCSE HISTORY WEBSITE APP AND MOBILE APP

GCSE History is a text and voice web and mobile app that allows you to easily revise for your GCSE/IGCSE exams wherever you are - it's like having your own personal GCSE history tutor. Whether you're at home or on the bus, GCSE History provides you with thousands of convenient bite-sized facts to help you pass your exams with flying colours. We cover all topics - with more than 120,000 questions - across the Edexcel, AQA and CIE exam boards.

GCSEHistory.com

GET IT ON
Google Play

Download on the
App Store

Contents

In this study guide, you will see a series of icons, highlighted words and page references. The key below will help you quickly establish what these mean and where to go for more information.

Icons

WHAT questions cover the key events and themes.

WHO questions cover the key people involved.

WHEN questions cover the timings of key events.

WHERE questions cover the locations of key moments.

WHY questions cover the reasons behind key events.

HOW questions take a closer look at the way in which events, situations and trends occur.

IMPORTANCE questions take a closer look at the significance of events, situations, and recurrent trends and themes.

DECISIONS questions take a closer look at choices made at events and situations during this era.

Highlighted words

abdicate - occasionally, you will see certain words highlighted within an answer. This means that, if you need it, you'll find an explanation of the word or phrase in the glossary which starts on **page 71**.

Page references

Tudor *(p.7)* - occasionally, a certain subject within an answer is covered in more depth on a different page. If you'd like to learn more about it, you can go directly to the page indicated.

Conflict and Tension between East and West 1945-1972 is a wider world depth study that investigates international relations. The course focuses on the causes and course of the Cold War. It considers why the conflict occurred, as well as how it developed into a global conflict over the following quarter of a century.

Purpose

This study will help you to understand the complexities and diverse interests of different states and how this affects the relationship between them. The course will enable you to analyse cause and consequence, making links between, and assessing the importance of, events in their historical context. It will also develop your critical evaluation skills.

Enquiries

Conflict and Tension 1945-72 is split into 3 key enquiries:

- 📖 Enquiry 1 examines the long and short term causes of the Cold War.
- 📖 Enquiry 2 looks at the development of the Cold War and how it increased international tension.
- 📖 Finally, enquiry 3 is a study of how key events led to a relaxation of tension in the Cold War.

Key Individuals

Some of the key individuals studied on this course include:

- 👤 Joseph Stalin.
- 👤 Franklin Roosevelt.
- 👤 Winston Churchill.
- 👤 Harry Truman.
- 👤 Mao Zedong.
- 👤 Nikita Khrushchev.
- 👤 Alexander Dubček.
- 👤 John F Kennedy.
- 👤 Leonid Brezhnev.

Key Events

Some of the key events and developments you will study on this course include:

- 🗓 The conferences after the Second World War.
- 🗓 The development of US and Soviet foreign policies.
- 🗓 The Berlin Blockade.
- 🗓 The Korean War.
- 🗓 The Vietnam War.
- 🗓 The space race.
- 🗓 The nuclear arms race.
- 🗓 The Berlin Wall.
- 🗓 The Cuban Missile Crisis.
- 🗓 The Prague Spring.
- 🗓 Detente.

Assessment

Conflict and Tension between East and West 1945-1972 is part of paper 1 (2 hours). You should spend 1 hour on this section of the paper. There will be 4 exam questions which will assess what you have learned from the course.

- 👥 Question 1 is worth 4 marks. This question will require you to examine a source, and explain its meaning in its historical context.
- 👥 Question 2 is worth 12 marks. This question will require you to examine 2 sources, and assesses your ability to evaluate sources for a particular purpose.
- 👥 Question 3 is worth 8 marks. It requires to you to explain and analyse historical events in relation to cause and consequence.

Quizzes, amazing exam preparation tools and more at GCSEHistory.com

Question 4 is worth 16 marks plus 4 marks for spelling, punctuation and grammar. Here you will be required to make a judgement about the importance of an event or development in an extended response.

Revision! A dreaded word. Everyone knows it's coming, everyone knows how much it helps with your exam performance, and everyone struggles to get started! We know you want to do the best you can in your GCSEs, but schools aren't always clear on the best way to revise. This can leave students wondering:

- ✓ How should I plan my revision time?
- ✓ How can I beat procrastination?
- ✓ What methods should I use? Flash cards? Re-reading my notes? Highlighting?

Luckily, you no longer need to guess at the answers. Education researchers have looked at all the available revision studies, and the jury is in. They've come up with some key pointers on the best ways to revise, as well as some thoughts on popular revision methods that aren't so helpful. The next few pages will help you understand what we know about the best revision methods.

How can I beat procrastination?

This is an age-old question, and it applies to adults as well! Have a look at our top three tips below.

⚙ Reward yourself

When we think a task we have to do is going to be boring, hard or uncomfortable, we often put if off and do something more 'fun' instead. But we often don't really enjoy the 'fun' activity because we feel guilty about avoiding what we should be doing. Instead, get your work done and promise yourself a reward after you complete it. Whatever treat you choose will seem all the sweeter, and you'll feel proud for doing something you found difficult. Just do it!

⚙ Just do it!

We tend to procrastinate when we think the task we have to do is going to be difficult or dull. The funny thing is, the most uncomfortable part is usually making ourselves sit down and start it in the first place. Once you begin, it's usually not nearly as bad as you anticipated.

⚙ Pomodoro technique

The pomodoro technique helps you trick your brain by telling it you only have to focus for a short time. Set a timer for 20 minutes and focus that whole period on your revision. Turn off your phone, clear your desk, and work. At the end of the 20 minutes, you get to take a break for five. Then, do another 20 minutes. You'll usually find your rhythm and it becomes easier to carry on because it's only for a short, defined chunk of time.

Spaced practice

We tend to arrange our revision into big blocks. For example, you might tell yourself: "This week I'll do all my revision for the Cold War, then next week I'll do the Medicine Through Time unit."

This is called **massed practice**, because all revision for a single topic is done as one big mass.

But there's a better way! Try **spaced practice** instead. Instead of putting all revision sessions for one topic into a single block, space them out. See the example below for how it works.

This means planning ahead, rather than leaving revision to the last minute - but the evidence strongly suggests it's worth it. You'll remember much more from your revision if you use **spaced practice** rather than organising it into big blocks. Whichever method you choose, though, remember to reward yourself with breaks.

Spaced practice (more effective):

week 1	week 2	week 3	week 4
Topic 1	Topic 1	Topic 1	Topic 1
Topic 2	Topic 2	Topic 2	Topic 2
Topic 3	Topic 3	Topic 3	Topic 3
Topic 4	Topic 4	Topic 4	Topic 4

Massed practice (less effective)

week 1	week 2	week 3	week 4
Topic 1	Topic 2	Topic 3	Topic 4

What methods should I use to revise?

Self-testing/flash cards	Self explanation/mind-mapping

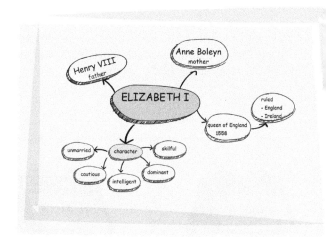

The research shows a clear winner for revision methods - **self-testing**. A good way to do this is with **flash cards**. Flash cards are really useful for helping you recall short – but important – pieces of information, like names and dates.

Side A - question

Side B - answer

Write questions on one side of the cards, and the answers on the back. This makes answering the questions and then testing yourself easy. Put all the cards you get right in a pile to one side, and only repeat the test with the ones you got wrong - this will force you to work on your weaker areas.

pile with right answers

pile with wrong answers

As this book has a quiz question structure itself, you can use it for this technique.

Another good revision method is **self-explanation**. This is where you explain how and why one piece of information from your course linked with another piece.

This can be done with **mind-maps**, where you draw the links and then write explanations for how they connect. For example, President Truman is connected with anti-communism because of the Truman Doctrine.

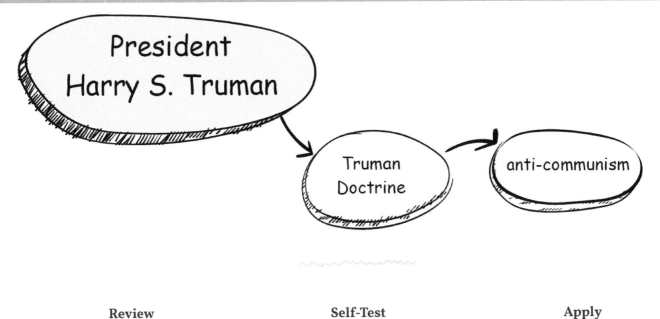

Review

Self-Test

Apply

Start by highlighting or re-reading to create your flashcards for self-testing.

Test yourself with flash cards. Make mind maps to explain the concepts.

Apply your knowledge on practice exam questions.

 Which revision techniques should I be cautious about?

Highlighting and **re-reading** are not necessarily bad strategies - but the research does say they're less effective than flash cards and mind-maps.

Highlighting

Re-reading

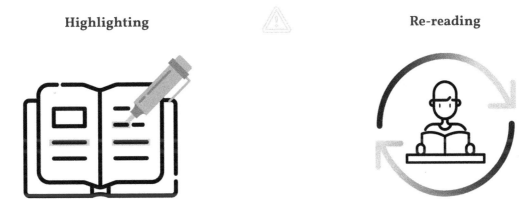

If you do use these methods, make sure they are **the first step to creating flash cards**. Really engage with the material as you go, rather than switching to autopilot.

TIMELINE

October 1917 - Communist revolution in Russia *(p.15)*

1917-1921 - Russian Civil War *(p.16)*

1917

1941

June 1941 - German invasion of USSR

1941 - Grand Alliance formed

1945

4-11 Feb 1945 - Yalta Conference *(p.18)*

July 1945 - USA tested atomic bomb *(p.18)*

17 July - 2 Aug 1945 - Potsdam Conference *(p.20)*

August 1945 - Atomic bombs dropped on Japan *(p.18)*

1945-1949 - Communist takeover of Eastern European states *(p.22)*

1946

February 1946 - Long Telegram *(p.21)*

March 1946 - Iron Curtain' speech *(p.27)*

March 1947 - Truman Doctrine announced *(p.29)*

1947

October 1947 - Cominform created *(p.30)*

1948

April 1948 - Marshall Plan began *(p.31)*

June 1948 - May 1949 - Berlin Blockade & Airlift *(p.33)*

June 1948 - Yugoslavia expelled from Cominform *(p.26)*

January 1949 - Comecon created *(p.32)*

1949

April 1949 - NATO created *(p.40)*

August 1949 - USSR tested atomic bomb *(p.43)*

October 1949 - People's Republic of China formed *(p.35)*

1950

June 1950 - July 1953 - Korean War *(p.36)*

USA tested hydrogen bomb *(p.44)*

1952

1953

March 1953 - Death of Stalin *(p.45)*

August 1953 - USSR tested hydrogen bomb *(p.44)*

Warsaw Pact created *(p.41)*

1955

1956

Feb 1956 - 'Secret Speech' began de-Stalinisation in USSR *(p.45)*

Oct - Nov 1956 - Hungarian Uprising *(p.46)*

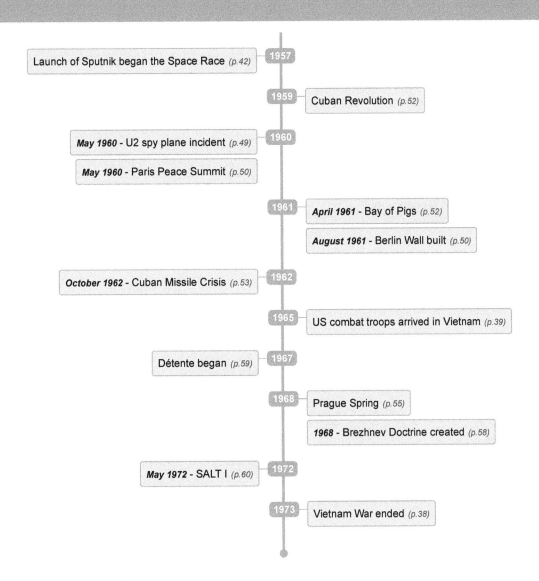

Launch of Sputnik began the Space Race *(p.42)* — **1957**

1959 — Cuban Revolution *(p.52)*

May 1960 - U2 spy plane incident *(p.49)* — **1960**

May 1960 - Paris Peace Summit *(p.50)*

1961 — *April 1961* - Bay of Pigs *(p.52)*

August 1961 - Berlin Wall built *(p.50)*

October 1962 - Cuban Missile Crisis *(p.53)* — **1962**

1965 — US combat troops arrived in Vietnam *(p.39)*

Détente began *(p.59)* — **1967**

1968 — Prague Spring *(p.55)*

1968 - Brezhnev Doctrine created *(p.58)*

May 1972 - SALT I *(p.60)* — **1972**

1973 — Vietnam War ended *(p.38)*

COLD WAR INTRODUCTION AND DEFINITION

'Let us not be deceived — we are today in the midst of a cold war. Our enemies are to be found abroad and at home.' Bernard Baruch 1947.

What was the Cold War?

The Cold War was a state of hostility that existed between the USSR and the USA in the second half of the 20th century.

What is the definition of a cold war?

A cold war is a conflict in which there is no direct fighting between the two sides. It is fought through economic and political actions.

When was the Cold War?

The Cold War lasted from 1945 to 1991.

Who was involved in the Cold War?

The Cold War was between the USA and its allies, and the Soviet Union, its satellite states and its allies.

What were the long-term causes of the Cold War?

There are 7 main reasons the Cold War happened:

- ☑ In October 1917, the Bolsheviks seized power in Russia. By 1921 they had created the first communist state. They were anti-capitalism and wanted to spread the communist revolution across the world.
- ☑ America and Britain did not trust the USSR as Russia had withdrawn from the First World War in 1917, despite being a member of the Triple Entente with Britain and France.
- ☑ The USSR did not trust the USA, France and Britain because they sent troops to fight against the Bolsheviks in the Russian Civil War *(p. 16)*.
- ☑ In the 1920s, the USA suffered from the First Red Scare and was hostile towards the USSR.
- ☑ The USSR was angry it was not recognised as a country by the USA until 1933.
- ☑ The relationship between the USSR and the West deteriorated before the Second World War. The Soviet Union was angry at not being invited to the Munich Conference in 1938.
- ☑ When the USSR signed the Nazi-Soviet Pact in 1939, Britain and France were horrified.

How was the Cold War fought?

The Cold War was fought in 7 key ways:

- ☑ Propaganda.
- ☑ Spying or espionage, such as using spy planes to take photographs.
- ☑ An arms race to have the most developed weapons, particularly nuclear missiles.
- ☑ A space race *(p.42)* competing for success in space, such as being the first nation to put a man on the moon.
- ☑ Financial aid or loans to other countries to gain their support.
- ☑ Proxy wars, where the USA and the USSR became involved in conflicts in other countries. An example is the Korean War *(p.36)* of 1950-53.
- ☑ Threats made by either side.

What created tension between the Soviet Union and the USA at the beginning of the Cold War?

The ideological differences between the superpowers created tension between them. The Soviet Union supported communism, whereas the USA and Britain were capitalist countries.

What were the different ideologies in the Cold War?

The Cold War was a result of ideological differences between the two sides:

- ☑ The USSR was communist. Communism is a system where there is no private ownership of land, property or business. The aim is to achieve economic equality for the benefit of the people through central control of the state economy.

- ☑ The USA was capitalist. Capitalism is a system where individuals are free to own land, property and businesses to create wealth and accept there will be economic inequality as a result.

Why were the USA and the USSR considered superpowers during the Cold War?

The USSR and the USA were considered to be superpowers because they possessed 3 key things:

- ☑ Massive military might, including nuclear weapons.
- ☑ Economic might.
- ☑ The ability to dominate other countries.

Why was Stalin distrustful of Truman at the beginning at the Cold War?

Joseph Stalin was distrustful of Harry S Truman for 3 key reasons:

- ☑ Truman was anti-communist.
- ☑ He tried to control the Potsdam meeting.
- ☑ He successfully tested the atomic bomb *(p.18)* without consulting Stalin and used it in the Hiroshima and Nagasaki bombings in the days after Potsdam.

Why did Britain ally closely with the USA at the beginning at the Cold War?

Britain was concerned about communism spreading. The nation's economy was severely impacted after the Second World War so it couldn't act against the Soviet Union alone.

DID YOU KNOW?

There is a lot of debate about when the Cold War really began - since it was never openly declared, we cannot put an exact date on it. Some suggest the American bombing of Hiroshima and Nagasaki; others suggest it goes right back to the Russian Revolution in 1917.

THE RUSSIAN REVOLUTION

'I suddenly realised that the devout Russian people no longer needed priests to pray them into heaven. On earth they were building a kingdom more bright than any heaven had to offer, and for which it was a glory to die' - John Reed, '10 Days that Shook the World'.

What was the Russian Revolution?

In 1917 the Bolshevik Party overthrew the Russian government and created the world's first communist state. Russia withdrew from the First World War and was plunged into civil war.

What was the impact of the Russian revolution on the Cold War?

The roots of the Cold War can be traced back to the Russian Revolution. It led to tension and distrust between the USSR and the USA which was brought to a head with the defeat of Hitler in 1945.

THE RUSSIAN CIVIL WAR

'Every person present here knows that perhaps this very evening they will be fighting in front of their own house, that they will perhaps be killed, that if they are taken alive they will be hanged, or shot, or tortured.' - Victor Serge

What was the Russian Civil War?

A civil war was triggered by opposition to the Bolsheviks from various groups, including monarchists who wanted the tsar back in power, anti-communists, groups angered by Brest-Litovsk and different nationalities who wanted their independence.

When was the Russian Civil War?

The Russian Civil War took place from 1918 to 1921.

Who fought in the Russian Civil War?

The Russian Civil War was fought between communist (Red) and anti-communist (White) forces. In addition, a number of countries, including Britain and the USA, sent troops to support the Whites. The Reds won.

What were the consequences of the Russian Civil War on international relations?

The Russian Civil War had 3 main consequences for international relations:

- ☑ It increased the Soviet Union's suspicion that the capitalist West would always seek to overthrow communism.
- ☑ In order to protect the USSR from future foreign interference, Lenin, the leader of the USSR, pursued a policy of worldwide communist revolution.
- ☑ This in turn caused a 'Red Scare' in 1920s America as many feared the worldwide spread of communism.

THE SECOND WORLD WAR AND THE COLD WAR

During the Second World War, the Grand Alliance forgot their differences and worked together to fight against Hitler. Without the Nazis as their common enemy, the alliance began to fall apart.

What was the impact of the Second World War on the Cold War?

After the German attack on the Soviet Union in 1941, the Russians joined the 'Grand Alliance' with Britain and the USA. The desire to defeat a common enemy meant that old suspicions were put aside. However, mistrust between the allies returned once the defeat of Hitler became inevitable, as both sides looked to influence the postwar world.

THE GRAND ALLIANCE
'The Russian danger ... is our danger' - Winston Churchill

What was the Grand Alliance?

The Grand Alliance was a military and political coalition against the Axis powers of Nazi Germany, Italy, and Japan during the Second World War.

When was the Grand Alliance formed?

The Grand Alliance began after the USA entered the Second World War. The alliance was formally signed by the USA, the Soviet Union and Great Britain on New Year's Day, 1942, and lasted until 1945.

Who was part of the Grand Alliance?

The Grand Alliance consisted of the three major Allies of the Second World War - the Soviet Union, the United States, and Great Britain.

Why was the Grand Alliance formed?

The sole purpose of the Grand Alliance was to defeat the Axis powers - Nazi Germany, fascist Italy and Imperial Japan.

Why was there tension in the Grand Alliance?

Although they were fighting the Nazi threat together, there were 3 main reasons for tension between the countries of the Grand Alliance during the Second World War:

- ☑ Both sides kept secrets. Stalin refused to share battle plans with Britain and France; when German troops surrendered in Italy, Britain and the US did not include the USSR in the discussions.
- ☑ Stalin believed the USA had deliberately delayed opening a second front in France until 1944 so the USSR would be weakened fighting Nazi Germany on its own.
- ☑ The two sides had opposing ideologies and did not trust each other.

How did the Grand Alliance cooperate during the Second World War?

The public was presented with a positive image of the Grand Alliance, and the three countries did help each other in 3 key ways:

- ☑ British merchant ships helped take supplies to the USSR.
- ☑ America included the USSR in its Lend-Lease programme, which meant it lent and sold military equipment to help defeat Germany.
- ☑ The USSR lost 26 million people fighting the Nazis after 1941, but this meant Germany's army was tied down and allowed Britain and America to plan and launch D-Day.

DID YOU KNOW?

The Grand Alliance is often referred to as a 'marriage of convenience'.

The USSR and the USA put aside their ideological differences to fight a common enemy, Nazi Germany.

HIROSHIMA AND NAGASAKI

'I am become death, the destroyer of worlds.' - Oppenheimer, a key scientist in the creation of the nuclear bomb, on witnessing a test detonation.

How did the atomic bomb affect the Cold War?

America's use of nuclear weapons against Japan in 1945 increased tension and distrust between the superpowers.

Why did America use nuclear weapons?

There is disagreement about why America did this. There are 2 main theories.

- The first theory says the Americans had no choice. Japan had been allied with Nazi Germany during the Second World War, and the USA believed the use of nuclear weapons would force the Japanese to surrender.
- The second theory is that the Americans did this as a way of showcasing their military power, to try to intimidate the Soviet Union before the coming Cold War.

Who ordered the nuclear bomb to be dropped in 1945?

President Harry Truman *(p.70)* authorised the use of nuclear weapons against Japan.

Which cities did the Americans attack with nuclear weapons?

The Americans launched nuclear attacks against the Japanese cities of Hiroshima and Nagasaki.

How many people died when the Americans used nuclear weapons against Japan?

Around 70,000 died in the initial blast at Hiroshima, and a further 40,000 at Nagasaki. Many more died over the coming weeks, months and years from severe burns and radiation poisoning.

How did the atomic bomb cause tension in the Cold War?

There were 3 key ways that dropping the nuclear bomb affected the Cold War.

- Truman had deliberately delayed the Potsdam meeting so that America could test the atomic bomb.
- Truman kept the existence of America's nuclear technology a secret until the attack and refused to share the technology. This created distrust and tension with the USSR.
- The dropping of the bomb made the USSR determined to possess its own nuclear weapon to even the stakes. This laid the ground for the later arms race between the superpowers.

DID YOU KNOW?

The USA is the only power ever to have deliberately used nuclear weapons against human targets.

THE YALTA CONFERENCE

The Yalta Conference was held to decide what would happen after the war.

What was the Yalta Conference?

The Yalta Conference was the second of three strategic meetings between the USA, Britain and the Soviet Union to discuss winning the war and post-war Europe.

Where was the Yalta Conference held?

The Yalta Conference took place in Yalta in the USSR.

When was the Yalta Conference held?

The Yalta Conference was held in February 1945.

Who attended the Yalta Conference?

The three Allied leaders present at the Yalta Conference were:

- ☑ President Roosevelt of the USA.
- ☑ General Secretary Stalin of the USSR.
- ☑ Prime Minister Churchill *(p.63)* of Great Britain.

What decisions were taken at the Yalta Conference?

There were 11 important decisions made at the Yalta Conference.

- ☑ The superpowers agreed on the Declaration of Liberated Europe which guaranteed all countries freed from Nazi control the right to hold democratic and free elections.
- ☑ Nazi Germany and Berlin would be divided into four zones controlled by the USA, Britain, France and the Soviet Union.
- ☑ Germany would be reduced in size.
- ☑ Germany would be demilitarised.
- ☑ Germany would be ordered to pay reparations.
- ☑ Nazi war criminals would be tried after the war was over and the Nazi Party banned.
- ☑ Poland would fall under the Soviet sphere of influence.
- ☑ Poland would be run under a democratically elected government.
- ☑ Eastern Europe would have free elections.
- ☑ The USSR would declare war on Japan 3 months after Nazi Germany was defeated.
- ☑ The United Nations was created.

What disagreements were there at the Yalta Conference?

There were 3 main disagreements at the Yalta Conference:

- ☑ The USSR wanted Germany to pay high reparations; Britain and the USA disagreed.
- ☑ Britain and the USA wanted Germany to recover, whereas the USSR wanted to keep Germany weak.
- ☑ Stalin wanted the Polish-German border to be much further to the west and desired a 'friendly' Polish government. Britain and the USA were worried this would mean Poland would be controlled by the USSR.

DID YOU KNOW?

The Yalta Conference was the final one that Stalin, Roosevelt and Churchill attended.

President Roosevelt died before the Potsdam Conference, and Churchill lost the general election to the Labour Party in July 1945.

THE POTSDAM CONFERENCE

The Potsdam Conference came a few months after Yalta. There was significant tension between the USSR and the USA over the issue of the atomic bomb.

What was the Potsdam Conference?

The Potsdam Conference was the third and final meeting between the USA, Britain and the Soviet Union to discuss Nazi Germany and the future of Europe.

Where was the Potsdam Conference held?

The Potsdam Conference was held in Potsdam, Germany.

When was the Potsdam Conference held?

The Potsdam Conference took place between July and August 1945.

Who attended the Potsdam Conference?

The three Allied leaders who met at Potsdam were:

- President Harry Truman *(p.70)* of the United States.
- Prime Minister Clement Attlee of Great Britain.
- Premier Joseph Stalin of the Soviet Union.

Why did the leaders at the Potsdam Conference change?

Leadership of two Allied nations had changed since the Yalta Conference *(p.18)*. Roosevelt died in April 1945 and Churchill *(p.63)* lost the British general election in July.

What disagreements were there at the Potsdam Conference?

There were 4 key areas of disagreement:

- The USA and Britain were unhappy Stalin had removed the non-communists from the Polish Provisional Government of National Unity.
- The USA and Britain were unhappy Stalin had not allowed free elections in eastern Europe. Stalin was angry as he thought the West was interfering.
- Truman deliberately delayed the Potsdam meeting so America could test the atomic bomb *(p.18)*. When Truman informed Stalin about the USA's successful test, Stalin was very angry not to have been told beforehand.
- Truman was very anti-communist and wanted to get 'tough' with Stalin.

What decisions were taken at the Potsdam Conference?

There were 8 important decisions made at the Potsdam Conference:

- The Nazi Party was banned.
- War criminals were to be prosecuted.
- Germany was to be reduced in size.
- Germany would be divided into four occupied zones controlled by the USA, Britain, France and the Soviet Union.
- Berlin would also be divided into four occupied zones controlled by the USA, Britain, France and the Soviet Union.
- All economic decisions about Germany must be agreed to by all four powers in the Allied Control Council.
- A Council of Foreign Ministers was set up to organise the rebuilding of Europe.
- It was decided the Soviet Union would receive 25% of the industrial output from the other three occupied zones.

THE LONG TELEGRAM

'It is clear that the main element of any United States policy towards the Soviet Union must be that of a long-term, patient but firm and vigilant containment of Russian expansive tendencies.' - George Kennan

What was the 'Long Telegram'?

The Long Telegram was a secret report sent by the US Ambassador in the Soviet Union, George Kennan, to President Truman.

When was the 'Long Telegram' sent?

The 'Long Telegram' was sent on 22nd February, 1946.

Who sent the 'Long Telegram'?

George Kennan, the US Ambassador in the Soviet Union, sent the 'Long Telegram'.

Where was the 'Long Telegram' sent?

The 'Long Telegram' was sent to Washington from the United States Embassy in Moscow.

What did the 'Long Telegram' say?

The 'Long Telegram' stated:

- ☑ The USSR was a threat to capitalism and should be eliminated.
- ☑ The USSR was building its military power.
- ☑ Peace between the USA and the USSR was not possible.
- ☑ The USSR was determined to expand.

SATELLITE STATES

After the Second World War, Stalin insisted on a protective 'buffer' of satellite states for the USSR.

What were the Soviet satellite states?

The Soviet satellite states were countries in eastern Europe under the political, economic and military influence of the USSR.

Who were the Soviet satellite states?

They were Poland, Czechoslovakia, Hungary, Romania, Bulgaria and East Germany.

When were the Soviet satellite states created?

The satellite states were created between 1946 and 1949.

What methods were used to create the Soviet satellite states?

There are 2 key things to note about the methods used:

- ☑ In the late 1940s, Stalin installed communist leaders in eastern European countries using 'salami tactics'.
- ☑ The term 'salami tactics' was coined by the communist Hungarian leader, Matyas Rakosi, to describe how Stalin dea with opposition 'slice by slice'.

How were the Soviet satellite states created?

There were 5 main ways in which the Soviet Union took over eastern European countries:

- ☑ The Red Army supported communists and intimidated the opposition. They acted as an occupying force.
- ☑ Elections were held and as a result the communists were part of coalition governments.
- ☑ The communists worked in coalitions to undermine the government and held key positions, such as head of the police, so they could arrest and murder opponents.
- ☑ Propaganda was used to label any opposition party or leader a fascist to boost support for communist parties or to demonise democratic politicians.
- ☑ Once in government, communist parties, aided by the security forces, rigged elections to ensure they remained in power.

What was the importance of the Soviet satellite states?

The satellite states helped the Soviet Union in 4 key ways:

- ☑ It meant the USSR had gained a large territory with which it could trade.
- ☑ They enhanced its power.
- ☑ In theory, they strengthened communism.
- ☑ They acted as a buffer zone to protect the USSR from invasion.

What were the different points of view about the Soviet satellite states?

There are 2 key things to note about how satellite states are viewed:

- ☑ Stalin viewed the satellite states as a necessary buffer against future invasion from Germany in particular.
- ☑ However, Britain and the USA saw them as a threat to the West.

POLAND

'Fitting communism onto Poland is like putting a saddle on a cow.'
- Stalin, 1944

What is Poland?

Poland is a country in central Europe.

When did Poland become a satellite state?

Soviet control was established over Poland in 1947.

How did Poland become a satellite state?

Poland became a satellite state through 5 key events:

- Before the Second World War, Poland had a mostly agricultural economy and a traditional hatred of the USSR.
- During the Second World War, it was at first divided between Germany and the USSR, and then completely occupied by Germany.
- During the war, it had two governments - one based in London, and the other in the Polish town of Lublin.
- After it was liberated, Soviet troops remained and a new government was formed in June 1945 dominated by communist-sympathising 'Lublin' Poles.
- Opposition leaders were assassinated and imprisoned before a rigged vote in 1947 gave the communists 80% of the vote.

CZECHOSLOVAKIA

'Victorious February!'
The name given to the month in which Czechoslovakia became communist.

What was Czechoslovakia?

Czechoslovakia was a country in central Europe.

When did Czechoslovakia become a satellite state?

Czechoslovakia came under Soviet control in 1948.

 ### How did Czechoslovakia become a satellite state?

Czechoslovakia became a satellite state through 5 key events:

- ☑ Czechoslovakia had a democracy and strong support for the communists before the war. It was invaded by Germany in 1939.
- ☑ After the war, Soviet troops left the country and elections put the communists in charge of a coalition government.
- ☑ The communists gradually took control of government ministries.
- ☑ Communists arrested political opponents and Jan Masaryk, a non-communist politician, was murdered in March 1948.
- ☑ All non-communist members of the government resigned in February 1948, and the communists assumed complete control.

DID YOU KNOW?

In March 1948, during a communist purge of the Czechoslovakian government, the pro-American foreign minister, Jans Masaryk, was found dead beneath his window.

Jan Masaryk expressed interest in Czechoslovakia receiving aid under the Marshall Plan. According to official reports he committed suicide by jumping from a window. A police report in 2004 ruled he was murdered.

HUNGARY

'Hungary conquered and in chains...' - Albert Camus

 ### What is Hungary?

Hungary is a landlocked country in central Europe.

 ### When did Hungary become a satellite state?

Soviet control was established over Hungary in 1948.

 ### How did Hungary become a satellite state?

Hungary became a satellite state through 6 key events:

- ☑ Hungary had an agricultural-based economy and little support for the communists. It was a German ally in the Second World War.
- ☑ Soviet troops remained in the country after liberation.
- ☑ In November 1945, elections gave communists 17% of the vote, but they were put in control of the Ministry of the Interior.
- ☑ They used secret police to control and intimidate opposition politicians.
- ☑ In 1947 rigged elections gave the communists control of the coalition government.
- ☑ The Social Democratic Party and Communist Party merged in 1948, giving the communists control of Hungary.

BULGARIA

'I feel deep anxiety because of...[the USSR's] overwhelming influence in the Balkans.' - Churchill to Truman, 1945

What is Bulgaria?

Bulgaria is a country in south-eastern Europe.

When did Bulgaria become a satellite state?

Bulgaria came under Soviet control in 1947.

How did Bulgaria become a satellite state?

Bulgaria became a satellite state through 5 key events:

- ☑ Before the Second World War, Bulgaria was a monarchy with strong links to Russia. However, during the war it was allied with Germany.
- ☑ Soviet troops remained there after the war.
- ☑ The communists joined the Fatherland Front, a coalition government with other parties. However, they then purged it of other political groups.
- ☑ The monarchy was abolished in 1946.
- ☑ In 1947 a new constitution destroyed democracy and outlawed opposition parties.

What was the Bulgaria dispute?

The Bulgaria Dispute was a crisis between Greece and Bulgaria following the killing of a Greek captain and soldier.

ROMANIA

'So far as Britain is concerned, how would it do for you to have 90% predominance in Romania, for us to have 90% of the say in Greece?' - Churchill to Stalin in 1944, in the so-called 'Percentages Agreement'

 ## What is Romania?

Romania is a south-eastern European country.

 ## When did Romania become a satellite state?

Soviet control was established in Romania in 1947.

 ## How did Romania become a satellite state?

Romania became a satellite state through 4 key events:

- Romania was a monarchy with little support for communism. During the Second World War it was a German ally.

- Soviet troops remained there after the war. The Soviets accepted a coalition government in 1945 with communists in key positions.

- The communists gradually took over the police, and rigged elections in 1946 gave them 90% of the vote.

- The main opposition leader was subject to a 'show trial' in October 1947 and King Michael was forced to abdicate.

DID YOU KNOW?

In 1945 and 1946, King Michael of Romania went on a 'royal strike' and refused to sign laws made by the communist government.

He was forced to abdicate shortly after attending the wedding of Queen Elizabeth II and Prince Philip in 1947.

YUGOSLAVIA

The leader of Yugoslavia, General Tito, was a communist but resisted control by the USSR.

 ## What was Yugoslavia?

Yugoslavia is a country in south east Europe. It was led by the communist Josip Tito from 1945 until his death in 1980.

 ## When did Yugoslavia become communist?

Yugoslavia became a communist state in 1945. It was unique amongst the countries of eastern Europe as it became communist independently and was therefore not a satellite state of the Soviet Union.

 ## What were relations like between Yugoslavia and the USSR?

At first, relations between Yugoslavia and the USSR were good. However, Yugoslavia's leader, Tito, repeatedly ignored Stalin as he was determined to implement communism in his own way. Things came to a head when Tito applied for Marshall Aid *(p.30)*.

Was Yugoslavia a member of Cominform?

Yugoslavia was a member of Cominform *(p.31)* until it was expelled in 1948 due to worsening relations with the USSR.

What was Yugoslavia's role in the Cold War?

Yugoslavia's position was unusual as the only communist state in Europe not behind the Iron Curtain. As a result, the USA gave it economic aid. However, it was a turbulent relationship as the state was too independent for the USA.

DID YOU KNOW?

Yugoslavia's own version of communism was called Titoism, after its leader.

The USSR produced more negative propaganda about General Tito during the Cold War than it did about America and the West.

THE IRON CURTAIN SPEECH, 1946

'From Stettin in the Baltic, to Trieste in the Adriatic, an iron curtain has descended across the continent' - Winston Churchill 1947.

What was the 'Iron Curtain' speech?

Winston Churchill *(p.63)*, although no longer the prime minister of Britain, gave a significant speech where he described how Europe had been divided by an 'iron curtain'. This analogy described the USSR's actions in eastern Europe that had divided Europe in two.

When was the 'Iron Curtain' speech delivered?

Winston Churchill *(p.63)* gave the speech in March 1946.

Who delivered the 'Iron Curtain' speech?

Winston Churchill *(p.63)* gave the 'Iron Curtain' speech.

Where was the 'Iron Curtain' speech delivered?

Winston Churchill *(p.63)* gave the speech in Fulton, USA.

What important argument was made by Churchill during the 'Iron Curtain' speech?

Churchill *(p.63)* argued that:

- ☑ Strong American-British relations were essential to stop the spread of communism and maintain peace.
- ☑ The USA must play an active role in world affairs.

Why was the 'Iron Curtain' speech important?

It helped bolster American and western European opposition to communism and the Soviet Union. It worsened relations between the USSR and the West.

How did Stalin respond to the 'Iron Curtain' speech?

Stalin responded to the 'Iron Curtain' speech by:

- ✅ Comparing Churchill *(p.63)* to Hitler and claiming Churchill was attempting to draw racial boundaries.
- ✅ Calling Churchill *(p.63)* a warmonger (someone who encourages or seeks war).

DID YOU KNOW?

Some regard Churchill's 'Iron Curtain' speech as the real beginning of the Cold War, because it was one of the first public announcements of hostility.

CONTAINMENT

Containment of communism became a key aim of American foreign policy from the 1940s onwards.

What was containment?

Containment was America's policy on communism. It involved preventing it from spreading to new countries, rather than attacking existing communist nations.

When was containment introduced?

Containment was first introduced in 1947.

What policy introduced the idea of containment?

Containment was first set out in the Truman Doctrine *(p.29)* and the Marshall Plan *(p.30)*.

What methods of containment were used?

The USA used 4 main methods of containment:

- ✅ It aimed to build bigger and better weapons faster than the USSR. This led to both sides becoming embroiled in an arms race.
- ✅ It offered economic support for countries threatened by communism.
- ✅ It forged alliances with other countries.
- ✅ It gave military assistance to countries threatened by communism.

Why was containment needed?

After the Second World War, the apparent need for containment was reinforced by 4 main global events:

- ✅ In 1947-48, eastern European countries were taken over by communist governments.
- ✅ In 1948, North Korea became communist.
- ✅ In August 1949, the USSR successfully tested an atomic bomb *(p.18)*.
- ✅ China became a communist country in 1949.

What alliances were formed as part of containment?

The USA formed 4 main alliances in response to the threat of communism:

- ✅ The most important was the North Atlantic Treaty Organisation, or NATO *(p.40)*, formed in 1949.

- The South-East Asia Treaty Organisation (SEATO) was formed in September 1954 between the USA, New Zealand, Australia, the Philippines, Thailand, Pakistan, Britain and France.
- CENTO, or the Central Treaty Organisation, was formed in February 1955 between Iran, Iraq, Pakistan, Turkey and the UK.
- The USSR responded by setting up the Warsaw Pact *(p.41)* in May 1955. The USSR, Romania, Bulgaria, Czechoslovakia, East Germany, Albania, Poland and Hungary were members.

How was military assistance used as part of containment?

The USA was prepared to provide weapons, military advice, training, troops, technical support and personnel to countries threatened by communism.

When was military assistance used as part of containment?

Examples of 3 significant occasions when the USA provided military support for countries threatened by communism were:

- 1950 - 1953 - in Korea, with UN support.
- 1961 - The Bay of Pigs invasion in Cuba.
- 1955 - 1975 - Vietnam.

THE TRUMAN DOCTRINE, 1947

'The seeds of totalitarian regimes are nurtured by misery and want. They spread and grow in the evil soil of poverty and strife.' - Harry Truman

What was the Truman Doctrine?

The Truman Doctrine was an American policy which was anti-communist and involved the containment of communism. It led to the Marshall Plan *(p.30)*.

When did the Truman Doctrine begin?

President Harry S Truman announced his doctrine on 12th March, 1947.

Why was the Truman Doctrine established?

There were 3 main reasons the Truman Doctrine was created:

- Britain could not afford to give any more military support to the Greek government in the civil war against Greek communists.
- The USA promised $400 million in aid to Greece and Turkey to help win the war against the Greek communists.
- It aimed to contain the spread of communism by giving military and economic assistance to any country threatened by communism.

What were the main points of the Truman Doctrine?

The Truman Doctrine contained 3 key points:

- It stated the world had a choice between communism, or capitalism and democracy;
- The USA would send troops and economic aid to countries threatened by communism so it was contained and could not spread;
- The USA would no longer follow an isolationist foreign policy and would now get involved in the affairs of other countries, rather than stay out of them.

What conditions were there in order for countries to receive aid under the Truman Doctrine?

Countries had to choose capitalism over communism in order to receive aid from the USA.

What was the importance of the Truman Doctrine?

There were 4 main reasons the Truman Doctrine was important:

- ☑ It meant the USA officially abandoned its isolationist foreign policy and would play an active role in the world.
- ☑ It meant the USA was on a potential collision course with the USSR as the doctrine was directed against the spread of communism.
- ☑ It directly resulted in the creation of the Marshall Plan *(p.30)*.
- ☑ It resulted in the further deterioration in the relationship between the USA and the USSR.

DID YOU KNOW?

The Truman Doctrine was the first American policy that expressed the need to contain the spread of communism.

THE MARSHALL PLAN, 1947

'Our policy is directed not against any country or doctrine but against hunger, poverty, desperation and chaos.' - Harry Truman

What was the Marshall Plan?

The Marshall Plan was a scheme to provide economic aid to Europe.

When was the Marshall Plan introduced?

The Marshall Plan was introduced in 1948.

Who came up with the Marshall Plan?

It was proposed by the US Secretary of State, George C Marshall.

Why was the Marshall Plan introduced?

The Marshall Plan was essentially the Truman Doctrine *(p.29)* in action. By making countries dependent on US dollars, it would prevent the spread of communism.

How much money was provided by the Marshall Plan?

$13.3 billion was provided by the USA to help rebuild Europe.

Which countries received aid under the Marshall Plan?

A total of 16 western European countries, including France, West Germany and Britain, received aid.

What was it hoped would be achieved by the Marshall Plan?

It was feared the damage and poverty caused by the Second World War would encourage people to turn to communism. Giving countries money to rebuild would stop them becoming communist.

Quizzes, amazing exam preparation tools and more at GCSEHistory.com

What were the conditions needed to receive aid from the Marshall Plan?

In order to receive money, countries had to trade with the USA and be capitalist.

 What was the reaction to the Marshall Plan?

The USSR reacted in 4 main ways to the Marshall Plan:

☑ The Soviet Union saw both the Truman Doctrine *(p.29)* and the Marshall Plan as a threat to communism.

☑ Stalin called it 'dollar imperialism' and claimed the USA was trying to take over Europe using its economic strength.

☑ Stalin responded by creating Cominform *(p.31)* in 1947, which coordinated and controlled communist parties in Europe from the USSR.

☑ Comecon *(p.32)* was established in 1949 to organise economic trade between eastern Europe and the USSR.

 What was the significance of the Marshall Plan?

The Marshall Plan was significant for 4 key reasons:

☑ It helped the economic recovery of western Europe.

☑ It limited the expansion of Soviet influence in Europe so the USSR was 'contained'.

☑ It deepened the divide between western Europe and eastern Europe as they were now divided politically and economically.

☑ It worsened the relationship between the USA and the USSR.

DID YOU KNOW?

If the USA spent the same proportion of its GDP on aid today as it did during the Marshall Plan, it would amount to $800 billion dollars.

COMINFORM

The Cominform described the world as divided into two sharply drawn camps, the camp of imperialism and war headed by the United States, and the camp of socialism and peace, headed by the Soviet Union.

 What was Cominform?

Cominform was the Communist Information Bureau. It organised all communist parties in Europe under the USSR's control.

 When was Cominform created?

The Communist Information Bureau was created in September 1947.

 Who were the members of Cominform?

Members included the USSR, France, Italy, Czechoslovakia, Bulgaria, Poland, Yugoslavia and Romania.

 Why was Cominform created?

Cominform was created for 2 key reasons:

☑ It was a reaction to the creation of the Marshall Plan *(p.30)* by the USA.

It was a way in which the USSR could control all communist parties in Europe.

Why was Cominform important?

Cominform meant that the USSR politically controlled all communist parties in eastern Europe. It created a trade network between communist countries.

DID YOU KNOW?

The leader of Yugoslavia, General Tito, resisted being controlled by Cominform.

As a result, he was expelled from the bureau in 1948.

COMECON

Comecon was seen as the Soviet 'answer' to the Marshall Plan.

What was Comecon?

Comecon was the Council for Mutual Economic Assistance. It was the Soviet Union's alternative to the Marshall Plan *(p.30)*.

When was Comecon created?

Comecon was created in January 1949.

Who was part of Comecon?

Comecon included the Soviet Union, Bulgaria, Czechoslovakia, Poland, Romania, Hungary, Albania and the German Democratic Republic (East Germany).

Why was Comecon created?

Comecon was a reaction to the Marshall Plan *(p.30)*, introduced by the USA, and was created for 2 main reasons:

 Stalin wanted to reduce any possible economic influence the USA could have on eastern Europe's communist countries by creating his own version of the Marshall Plan *(p.30)*.

 It was a method of controlling the satellite states in eastern Europe by tying them into close trading relationships with the USSR and each other.

What was the importance of Comecon?

Comecon, with the Marshall Plan *(p.30)*, divided Europe into two economic spheres of influence; western European was capitalist and eastern European was communist.

DID YOU KNOW?

Comecon was used to develop closer ties between the USSR and the countries of eastern Europe.

Quizzes, amazing exam preparation tools and more at GCSEHistory.com

THE BERLIN BLOCKADE, 1948-9

The Berlin Blockade was seen as an aggressive move by Stalin, designed to establish dominance over Berlin and Germany.

What was the Berlin Blockade?

The USSR closed all road, rail and river transport links into West Berlin. This stopped all supplies getting into the city. British, French and US troops were asked to leave.

When was the Berlin Blockade?

The Berlin Blockade started in June 1948 and ended in May 1949.

What caused the Berlin Blockade?

There were 8 key causes of the Berlin Blockade:

- ☑ The growing tension between the USA and the USSR over the future of Germany.
- ☑ The growing tension between the USA and the USSR because of their ideological differences and the start of the Cold War.
- ☑ In January 1947, the British and USA joined their zones, creating 'Bizonia'. This broke the agreements made at the Potsdam Conference *(p.20)*.
- ☑ In December 1947, at the London Conference, Britain, France and the USA met to discuss Germany and decide Germany's new constitution. The USSR was not included.
- ☑ In March 1948, France's zone joined Bizonia to create 'Trizonia'.
- ☑ The USSR left the Allied Control Commission, accusing the West of breaking the Potsdam agreements. They were angry the London Conference had taken place.
- ☑ In April 1948, Trizonia started to receive Marshall Aid *(p.30)* and began to rebuild.
- ☑ Britain, France and the USA introduced a new 'safe' currency, the Deutschmark, into Trizonia on 23rd June, 1948, which angered the USSR.

What were the consequences of the Berlin Blockade?

There were 3 main consequences of the Berlin Blockade:

- ☑ It prevented supplies reaching West Berlin.
- ☑ It led to the Berlin Airlift *(p.34)* from June 1948 to May 1949, in which the Western powers used airplanes to fly supplies into West Berlin.
- ☑ The relationship between the USSR and the West deteriorated further, eventually leading to the creation of NATO *(p.40)*.

What was the significance of the Berlin Blockade?

The Berlin Blockade was significant for 2 key reasons:

- ☑ The West saw it as an act of aggression by Stalin.
- ☑ It created the first major crisis between the USA and the USSR in the Cold War.

DID YOU KNOW?

The blockade lasted 318 days (11 months).

THE BERLIN AIRLIFT

Rather than risk war over the Berlin Blockade, the Americans got around it with the Berlin Airlift.

What did the western powers do in response to the Berlin Blockade?

Western powers responded to the blockade of West Berlin by organising an airlift. Supplies were flown into West Berlin every day.

When was the Berlin Airlift?

The Berlin Airlift saw supplies flown into Berlin every day from 26th June, 1948, to 12th May, 1949.

Why did the Berlin Airlift happen?

There were 3 main reasons the Berlin Airlift occurred:

☑ The West did not want to be forced out of West Berlin because Stalin would be able to take over.

☑ The USA wanted to contain communism, as promised in the Truman Doctrine *(p.29)*.

☑ It was a way to get around the blockade without starting a war.

What happened during the Berlin Airlift?

There were 3 key events during the Berlin Airlift:

☑ Britain, France and the USA flew in supplies of food, medicine and fuel throughout the Blockade.

☑ By the end of the Blockade, approximately 8,000 tonnes of supplies were being flown in every day.

☑ A new airport called Berlin-Tegel was built and a new runway was built at Berlin-Tempelhof to cope with the number of planes flying in supplies.

What were the consequences of the Berlin Airlift?

There were 4 key consequences of the Berlin Airlift:

☑ Two Germanies were created; The Federal Republic of Germany (West Germany) in May 1949 and the German Democratic Republic (East Germany) in October 1949.

☑ It led to the USA creating a military alliance called NATO *(p.40)* in April 1949.

☑ Europe was divided even more: politically (capitalism versus communism), economically (Marshall Aid *(p.30)* versus Comecon *(p.32)*), and now militarily.

☑ The balance of power became more unstable when the USSR conducted its first successful atomic bomb *(p.18)* test in August 1949.

DID YOU KNOW?

The Americans airlifted a total of 2,245,315 tons of supplies into Berlin during the airlift.

An Allied plane landed in Berlin every minute.

CHINA

'Classes struggle, some classes triumph, others are eliminated. Such is history; such is the history of civilization for thousands of years.' - Mao Zedong, in an article written in August 1949.

What is communist China?

After the Second World War, China became the 'People's Republic of China', a communist state. This added a new dimension to the Cold War conflict.

When did China become a communist country?

China became a communist country in 1949.

Who was the leader of communist China?

The new leader of communist China was Mao Zedong.

What events led to China becoming communist?

There were 5 main events that led to China becoming a communist country.

- ☑ The Chinese empire came to an end in 1911. The country became a republic, and rival factions fought to determine China's future.
- ☑ In July 1921, the Chinese Communist Party was formed, led by Mao Zedong. Support grew among many people in China, especially from the majority peasant population.
- ☑ From the 1920s, Chinese communists fought a civil war with Chiang Kai-shek's nationalist party, the Kuomintang (KMT).
- ☑ During the Second World War, the two parties joined forces to fight Japan, but the conflict renewed when the war ended.
- ☑ Despite US support for the KMT, the communists were eventually victorious. On 1st October, 1949, Mao Zedong announced the establishment of the People's Republic of China.

How did China becoming communist affect the Cold War?

The fall of China to communism was an important development in the Cold War, turning it from a predominantly European conflict into a worldwide struggle.

How did China becoming communist cause tension in the Cold War?

The fall of China to communism caused tension between the superpowers in 3 main ways.

- ☑ It represented a huge failure of President Truman's containment policy *(p.28)*. The USSR now had a communist ally in Asia.
- ☑ The Treaty of Friendship was agreed in 1950, committing the USSR to support China's economic, technological and military development. The USA saw this as an attempt by Stalin to spread communism worldwide.
- ☑ The USA refused to recognise the new regime as China's legitimate government, and continued to support Chiang Kai-shek's right to represent China in the UN.

DID YOU KNOW?

The Communist Party still rules in China to this day.

THE KOREAN WAR

The Korean War was a major escalation of Cold War tensions, and only narrowly avoided the use of nuclear weapons.

What was the Korean War?

The Korean War was fought between North and South Korea and was the first flashpoint of the Cold War in Asia.

Where did the Korean War take place?

In Korea, which is between China to the west and Japan to the east.

When was the Korean War?

The Korean War began in June 1950 and finished in 1954.

What were the key phases of the Korean War?

There were 5 main phases to the war, including:

☑ North Korea invaded South Korea on 25th June, 1950.

☑ A UN army, made up mostly of American military and led by General Douglas MacArthur, arrived in Korea in September 1950 to push back against the North Korean invasion.

☑ In October 1950, UN forces advanced into North Korean territory.

☑ On 25th October, China entered the war. Together with the North Korean army, they pushed the UN forces back below the 38th parallel. This resulted in a stalemate for over two years.

☑ After peace talks on 27th July, 1953, the UN, China and North Korea signed a peace treaty.

What were the long-term causes that led to the Korean War?

Several important long-term events led to the Korean War, including:

☑ The history of Korea was shaped by many wars over who would control it. Both China and Japan ruled the nation for significant periods of time.

☑ Between 1910 and 1945, Korea was controlled by Japan. This changed at the end of the Second World War.

☑ At the end of the Second World War, the Japanese in the north surrendered to the USSR, and those in the south to the USA.

At the end of the Second World War, what was the situation that led to the Korean War?

At the end of the Second World War, when Japan surrendered and Korea was occupied by Soviet troops in the north and American troops in the south, the following happened:

☑ The country was divided into two separate zones along the 38th parallel, a circle of latitude that runs across the middle of Korea.

☑ The division of Korea was supposed to be temporary. The aim was for it to be a united and independent country. The United Nations was to organise elections that would achieve this.

☑ Instead of free elections, the Soviets in North Korea enabled Korean communist Kim II-Sung to take control of the nation without being elected.

☑ There was an election in US-controlled South Korea, and USA supporter and capitalist figure Syngman Rhee became its leader.

☑ At this point, North and South Korea became two different nations. The USSR zone in the north became the People's Republic of Korea, and the US zone in the south became the Republic of Korea.

☑ While the leaders in both North and South Korea were nationalists and wanted a united country after the war, they wanted the nation to be led by different ideologies - capitalism in the south and communism in the north.

Who ran North Korea at the time of the Korean War?

After 1947, the government in North Korea was the communist Democratic People's Republic led by Kim Il-Sung. The capital was Pyongyang.

Who ran South Korea at the time of the Korean War?

After 1947, the government in South Korea was the non-communist Republic of Korea led by Syngman Rhee. Its capital was Seoul.

What were the key events in the build-up to the Korean War?

The leaders of North and South Korea each saw themselves as the legitimate and rightful ruler of the whole nation. Events in the build-up to the Korean War included:

- ☑ Due to the attitude of superiority from both sides there were a number of clashes on the border between North and South Korea.
- ☑ Kim Il-Sung, the leader of North Korea, visited Stalin in 1949 to ask for his support in an invasion of South Korea. He felt this would be welcome in the south as an effort to reunite the two nations.
- ☑ Stalin did not think it was the right time as he did not want a fight against US troops still stationed in South Korea.
- ☑ In 1950, Stalin's circumstances had changed. The US troops had left South Korea; communists were in power in China; and the USSR had its own nuclear weapons and had cracked the secret codes used by the USA to talk to other nations. As a result, Stalin felt any future actions in Korea would not meet American opposition.
- ☑ Stalin began sending tanks, artillery and aircraft to North Korea and gave the go-ahead for an invasion of the south.
- ☑ Stalin stated USSR soldiers would not be directly involved, and if further supplies were needed North Korea should ask China.

What started the Korean War?

The Korean War broke out when North Korea invaded South Korea on 25th June, 1950.

Why did the UN get involved in the Korean War?

When the south was invaded, the USA brought the matter to the UN which passed a resolution calling for North Korea to withdraw. When it did not, the UN sent international troops - mostly American - to force it out. In this way the USA could argue it was acting against international aggression rather than following its containment policy (p.28).

Why did America get involved in the Korean War?

There were 3 key reasons America got involved in the Korean War:

- ☑ President Truman was concerned communism was spreading in Asia.
- ☑ China's fall to communism in 1949 heightened this fear.
- ☑ Truman was also concerned about Stalin's use of Cominform (p.31) to encourage countries to turn to communism.

What was America's role in the Korean War?

America had 2 main roles in the Korean War:

- ☑ United Nations troops, mainly American and led by US General Douglas MacArthur, were sent to Korea. The North was supported by the Soviet Union.
- ☑ UN forces were able to push North Korea back to the Chinese border, but in late 1950 China joined the war and the UN had to retreat.

What ended the Korean War?

After three years of fighting an armistice was agreed, which re-established the border between North and South Korea.

What effect did the Korean War have on America?

There were 5 main consequences of the Korean War:

- ☑ It demonstrated the USA's commitment to containing communism and led to a tripling of military spending to prevent its spread.

- ☑ To stop the spread of communism in Asia, the Southeast Asia Treaty Organisation (SEATO) was set up in September 1954. Britain, Pakistan, USA, Thailand, France, Australia, the Philippines and New Zealand all joined.

- ☑ The sacking of General MacArthur over his proposal to deploy nuclear bombs against North Korea underlined the USA's caution with regard to using nuclear weapons.

- ☑ The Soviet Union doubled the size of the Red Army, from 2.8 million in 1950 to 5.6 million in 1955.

- ☑ As the war did not escalate further, it showed neither superpower was prepared to engage in direct military confrontation with the other, preferring instead to fight proxy wars.

DID YOU KNOW?

The Korean War, with approximately three million fatalities, was the first time the Cold War turned 'hot' and broke out into actual violence.

THE VIETNAM WAR

'If we are driven from the field in Vietnam, then no nation can ever again have the same confidence in American promise or protection ... We did not choose to be the guardians at the gate, but there is no one else.' - Lyndon Johnson, in a speech of July 1965.

What was the Vietnam War?

The Vietnam War was a lengthy conflict which began in 1954, after Vietnam was divided into two. North Vietnam wanted to reunite the country under communism while South Vietnam, assisted by the USA, fought to keep this from happening.

When did the Vietnam War happen?

Officially the Vietnam War began in 1955 and ended in 1975. However, some events prior to 1955 are important in order to understand how the war developed.

What were the key phases in the Vietnam War?

There were 4 key phases to the Vietnam War, including:

- ☑ The 1st phase of the conflict was between 1945 and 1954. The Vietminh fought to drive French imperial rule from Vietnam. This ended with the signing of the Geneva Accords and Vietnam being split into 2 countries. This period is called the First Indochina War.

- ☑ The 2nd phase, between 1957 and 1963, saw the leader of South Vietnam, Ngo Dinh Diem, fight a bitter civil war against the Vietcong which was supported by Ho Chi Minh's government in the north. This ended with Diem being assassinated just weeks before the American president, John F Kennedy, was assassinated in November 1963.

- ☑ The 3rd phase, from 1964 to 1968, saw a huge escalation in the conflict between America - which before 1964 had no direct military presence in the region - and North Vietnam. America was fighting the Vietcong directly in order to stop a communist takeover in the south.

- ☑ The 4th phase of the conflict, between 1969 and 1973, was defined by America's desire to withdraw from Vietnam and its actions to bring US troops home. The last military personnel were withdrawn from the region in 1973.

Who was involved in the Vietnam War?

There were a number of different parties and nations involved in the war including:

- France - the roots of the conflict begin with its attempts to maintain rule in Vietnam after the Second World War.
- Ho Chi Minh's Vietminh, which fought to remove all foreign influences from Vietnam. After the division of the country in 1954, under the Geneva Accords, Ho Chi Minh would become the leader of North Vietnam. Much of the war featured his battles with the Americans as he tried to take over South Vietnam and unite the two nations.
- The USA was involved in the conflict from July 1950, when it tried to assist the French against the Vietminh.
- Both China and the USSR were involved, supporting Ho Chi Minh from the start of conflict as he tried to drive out the French.
- South Vietnam was a new country created in 1954 under the Geneva Accords, and America's presence there was a bid to stop a communist takeover.
- Cambodia and Laos were drawn into the conflict on occasions, due to shared borders with Vietnam.

What was the role of France in the Vietnam War?

From 1945, the French had fought to keep control of its colonies in Indochina. In Vietnam, over 50,000 French soldiers had been killed as France fought against the Vietminh for 8 years.

What was the background to the Vietnam War?

In 1954, a peace agreement was signed in Geneva between the French and the Vietnamese. Vietnam was divided into communist North Vietnam and US-backed South Vietnam. In 1960 a guerrilla organisation, the Vietcong, was formed in the south. Its aim was to overthrow Diem, the region's leader, and unite the whole of Vietnam under communist rule.

Why did the USA get involved in the Vietnam War?

The USA was concerned about the Domino Theory and could not allow South Vietnam to become communist. It became increasingly involved in supporting South Vietnam as part of its containment policy *(p.28)*.

How did the USA get involved in the Vietnam War?

There were 3 key stages to American involvement in the Vietnam War:

- From 1950, the USA gave $1.6 billion dollars in aid to South Vietnam, and sent political advisers.
- From 1960, it began to send military advisers to train the South Vietnamese Army.
- From 1965, it sent American combat troops to Vietnam and became fully involved in the war.

Which US presidents got involved in the Vietnam War?

The USA's involvement in Vietnam spanned 5 different presidents:

- President Truman, who started sending military aid to the French to fight the Vietminh.
- President Eisenhower, who was the first to send military aid to the new South Vietnamese government in January 1955.
- President Kennedy *(p.66)*, who began increasing the number of US military advisors sent to Vietnam to train the ARVN - the South Vietnamese army.
- President Johnson, who committed the first US boots on the ground to Vietnam in March 1965.
- President Nixon, who led the withdrawal of all American troops from Vietnam.

How did the Vietnam War affect the Cold War?

The Vietnam War had an impact on the Cold War in 3 main ways:

- It was a humiliating defeat for the USA. The world's greatest superpower had been beaten by a small, under-equipped, yet committed guerrilla army. It influenced US involvement in future conflicts.

It was a failure of the containment policy *(p.28)*, as Vietnam was now united under communist leadership. Laos and Cambodia followed suit in 1975.

 Ironically, it helped lead to greater cooperation between the superpowers, as the USA sought the Soviet Union's help in ending the war.

What was the cost of the Vietnam War?

The Vietnam War cost much more than anticipated - a total of $167 billion.

What was Congress's response to the Vietnam War after the invasion of Cambodia?

Congress responded to the Vietnam War in 4 important ways after the invasion of Cambodia in 1970.

 The Gulf of Tonkin Resolution was revoked.

Military funding was limited.

A cut-off date of 30th June 1970 was set for troops to leave Cambodia.

A deadline of December 1971 was set for the total withdrawal of US troops from Vietnam.

What were the reasons for the Vietnam War being unwinnable?

Many historians argue the Vietnam War was unwinnable for 9 key reasons:

North Vietnam was determined to withstand the USA.

The US military struggled to defeat the Vietcong's guerrilla tactics.

The war had to stay within limits if the USA was to avoid confrontation with China or the USSR.

The Americans knew little about the country.

Vietnamese peasants were alienated by American policy, and the tactics used by the US military.

Vietnam had a history of opposing conquering countries, such as France and Japan.

The USA was unable to close the Ho Chi Minh Trail, which was used to supply the Vietcong.

American soldiers were unused to jungle warfare, while the Vietnamese were experts.

The South Vietnamese government had been unstable ever since the death of Diem in 1963.

DID YOU KNOW?

There were huge protests in the USA against the Vietnam War, which played a role in the USA's eventual defeat in Vietnam.

NATO

'The North Atlantic Treaty Organisation is first and foremost an effective defence alliance. It prevents potential opponents from being tempted to exert political pressure on any one of the allies through military force.' - Willy Brandt, 1968.

What is NATO?

NATO is an acronym for North Atlantic Treaty Organisation. It is a military alliance based on the promise of mutual defence against an attack by an external force.

When was NATO formed?

NATO was formed on 4th April, 1949.

Quizzes, amazing exam preparation tools and more at GCSEHistory.com

Who joined NATO?

The original 12 members were: the USA, Canada, Great Britain, Belgium, France, Italy, the Netherlands, Norway, Denmark, Luxembourg, Portugal and Iceland.

Why was NATO created?

NATO was formed by the USA and other western countries for 2 main reasons:

- ☑ Stalin and USSR's actions in the Berlin Blockade *(p.33)* had worried them.
- ☑ They wanted military protection from future aggression.

What were the consequences of the creation of NATO?

There were 4 key consequences of the creation of NATO:

- ☑ The USSR was contained in Europe, ensuring if it attacked any European member of NATO the other members would help the country under attack.
- ☑ All NATO members were protected by the promise of mutual military aid against any Soviet attack, helping to make the security of western Europe stronger.
- ☑ In response to West Germany joining NATO, the Soviet Union formed the Warsaw Pact *(p.41)* in 1955 so the USSR had full military control over eastern Europe.
- ☑ The USA had committed to a military presence in Europe.

What message was sent by the creation of NATO?

The creation of NATO sent 2 main messages to the USSR:

- ☑ The USA and western European countries would not accept Soviet aggression.
- ☑ The West would maintain the idea of containment set out in the Truman Doctrine *(p.29)*.

Why was NATO important?

NATO was important for 2 main reasons:

- ☑ It was based on the idea of 'collective security' - when one country is attacked, the rest must assist it.
- ☑ It acted as a deterrent to a military attack by the Soviet Union on western Europe.

DID YOU KNOW?

NATO still exists today.

THE WARSAW PACT

The Warsaw Pact was the Soviet answer to the North Atlantic Treaty Organisation - they hurried to form it after West Germany joined NATO.

What was the Warsaw Pact?

The Warsaw Pact was a defensive military alliance between the USSR and eastern European countries.

When was the Warsaw Pact signed?

The Warsaw Pact was established on 14th May, 1955.

Who was part of the Warsaw Pact?

The members of the Warsaw Pact were the USSR, Albania, Bulgaria, Czechoslovakia, East Germany, Hungary, Poland and Romania.

Why was the Warsaw Pact created?

There were 2 key reasons the Warsaw Pact was created:

- The USSR felt threatened when West Germany was allowed to join NATO *(p.40)* in 1955 because Germany had invad Russia in both world wars.
- The Pact would increase the USSR's control over eastern Europe.

What did the members of the Warsaw Pact agree to?

By joining the Warsaw Pact, members agreed to defend each other if they were attacked by a non-member. This was th idea of collective security.

What were the consequences of the creation of the Warsaw Pact?

There were 3 main consequences of the creation of the Warsaw Pact:

- The USSR increased control over the satellite states in eastern Europe because it dominated the Pact.
- Europe was now divided politically, economically and militarily into two hostile camps.
- It intensified the arms race with the West.

DID YOU KNOW?

The USSR heavily prioritised the Warsaw Pact - during the Hungarian Uprising of 1956, it was the Hungarian government's attempt to leave the Warsaw Pact that provoked the Soviets to invade.

THE SPACE RACE

'I would like to devote this first space flight to the people of communism, a society into which our Soviet people is already entering and into which, I am sure, all people on Earth will enter.' - Yuri Gagarin, first man in space.

What was the Space Race?

The Space Race was a struggle between the Soviet Union and the USA to be the first to achieve key milestones in the exploration of space - including the launch of the first artificial satellite, sending the first living creature into space, an sending the first human being into space.

Why was there a Space Race?

There were two main reasons why the Space Race happened.

- Both superpowers wanted to prove the superiority of their ideology, by showing that they could develop space trav more quickly than the other.

- [x] Each superpower was concerned that its rival would gain a military advantage in space, especially by being able to launch nuclear ICBMs from space.

What happened in the Space Race?

There were 5 major milestones in the Space Race.

- [x] In October 1957, the Soviets launched Sputnik - the first man-made satellite - into space. This was seen as a huge victory for communism.
- [x] In November 1957, the Soviets put the first living creature into space - a dog named Laika.
- [x] In August 1961, Soviet cosmonaut Yuri Gagarin became the first man in space.
- [x] In July 1963, Soviet cosmonaut Valentina Tereshkova became the first woman in space.
- [x] In July 1969, American astronaut Neil Armstrong became the first man to walk on the moon.

Which side won the Space Race?

Although Neil Armstrong's moon landing is arguably the best-remembered event, the Soviet Union achieved almost all other major milestones first. By 1975, the two superpowers had begun to cooperate, and they launched a joint space flight as part of the Apollo-Soyuz project.

> ### DID YOU KNOW?
> The Russian word 'sputnik' means 'fellow-traveller'.

THE ARMS RACE

'I think the bomb instead constitutes merely a first step in a new control by man over the forces of nature too revolutionary and dangerous to fit into old concepts.' - Henry Stimson

What was the arms race?

The arms race was a competition between the USA and the USSR to gain military dominance by developing their nuclear capabilities and weapons.

When was the arms race?

The Soviet Union emerged as a nuclear power in 1949, leading to the arms race with the USA. This lasted until the end of the Cold War in 1990.

What was the importance of the arms race?

The arms race was important for 2 main reasons:

- [x] It led to the fear of mutually assured destruction as both sides had enough weapons to destroy the world many times over.
- [x] The USA and the USSR had to find ways to solve disputes that did not result in a nuclear war.

What were the most important events of the arms race?

There were 6 main military achievements and events during the arms race:

- [x] 1945 - the USA dropped atomic bombs on Hiroshima and Nagasaki, bringing the Second World War to an end.
- [x] 1949 - the USSR tested an atomic bomb *(p. 18)*.

- ☑ 1952 - the USA developed the hydrogen bomb.
- ☑ 1953 - the USSR tested its own hydrogen bomb.
- ☑ 1957 - both the USA and USSR successfully tested intercontinental ballistic missiles (ICBMs).
- ☑ 1962 - the Cuban Missile Crisis *(p.53)* was the highest point of tension in the arms race.

What role did brinkmanship play in the arms race?

Brinkmanship was important in the arms race because:

- ☑ An enemy could be forced to back down in a moment of crisis by pushing it to the brink of an unwanted war.
- ☑ To make any threats credible, both sides needed nuclear weapons.
- ☑ The Cuban Missile Crisis *(p.53)* is an example of brinkmanship. The USA and the USSR were very close to a nuclear war, with both sides threatening conflict until the USSR backed down.

What was the theory of mutually assured destruction, or MAD in the arms race?

Mutually assured destruction, or MAD, was the following theory:

- ☑ It had developed by the 1960s.
- ☑ It stated that if either the USA or the USSR used their nuclear weapons, both would be destroyed. Each possessed so many, the damage would be unimaginable.
- ☑ It was believed war would be prevented because both sides feared it; a nuclear war was, in theory, unwinnable.

What were intercontinental ballistic missiles in the arms race?

Intercontinental ballistic missiles, called ICBMs, were nuclear-armed ballistic missiles with a range of more than 3,500 miles.

What were anti-ballistic missiles in the arms race?

Anti-ballistic missiles were missiles that would intercept and destroy other ballistic missiles. The USA and the USSR developed ABMs in the 1960s.

What were multiple independent reentry vehicles in the arms race?

Multiple independent reentry vehicles (MIRVs) were developed in 1968. These missiles carried multiple warheads which could each be independently targeted.

DID YOU KNOW?

In October 1961, the USSR tested its largest nuclear weapon, the Tsar Bomba, creating the most powerful man-made explosion ever seen.

The explosion yielded 58 megatons of TNT and blast waves were recorded as travelling three times around the earth.

DE-STALINISATION

Khrushchev briefly appeared to be calming the Cold War down with his policies of destalinisation and 'peaceful coexistence'.

What was De-Stalinisation?

De-Stalinisation was a series of political reforms in the USSR which were introduced after the death of Stalin in 1953.

When did De-Stalinisation happen?

De-Stalinisation took place from 1956 to 1964.

Who introduced De-Stalinisation?

Khrushchev brought in the policy of De-Stalinisation in his 'Secret Speech'.

What did the 'Secret Speech' say about Stalin's government during the period of De-Stalinisation?

Khrushchev's 'Secret Speech' criticised the brutality of Stalin's government and led people to believe Soviet control would be relaxed in eastern Europe.

Why was De-Stalinisation introduced?

There were 3 possible reasons why Khrushchev brought in his policy of De-Stalinisation:

- ☑ To weaken the position of his political rivals inside the USSR's Communist Party.
- ☑ To weaken the secret police and the Gulag system.
- ☑ To help develop peaceful coexistence with the USA, with the idea the USSR would not interfere in America's affairs.

What was the impact of De-Stalinisation on the Cold War?

De-Stalinisation influenced the Cold War in 3 main ways:

- ☑ It was seen as a time when the relationship between the USA and the USSR improved - there was a 'thaw' in the Cold War.
- ☑ When the contents of the 'Secret Speech' reached eastern Europe, people expected the repressive nature of communist-controlled governments would be relaxed.
- ☑ It encouraged rebellions in Hungary and, later, Czechoslovakia.

DID YOU KNOW?

Many hardline communists were furious with Khrushchev for tarnishing Stalin's legacy.

HUNGARY, 1956

'The 5,000 students who were meeting in front of the Petofi Monument in Budapest were joined shortly after dusk by thousands of workers and others. The great crowd then marched to the Stalin monument. Ropes were wound round the statue's neck, and, to cheers, the crowd attempted to topple the statue.' - The Manchester Guardian, 1956

 ### What was the Hungarian Uprising?

The Hungarian people demonstrated against communist rule. Prime Minister Imre Nagy ended one-party rule and announced that Hungary would leave the Warsaw Pact *(p.41)*.

 ### When did the Hungarian Uprising happen?

The uprising in Hungary happened between July and October, 1956.

 ### Why did the Hungarian Uprising happen?

There were 4 main causes of the Hungarian Uprising:

- ☑ Since 1949 the USSR had taken industrial and agricultural goods away from Hungary, and as a result Hungary was very poor.
- ☑ Hungary's Prime Minister, Matyas Rakosi, was a hard-line communist and had crushed all political opposition in Hungary.
- ☑ Khrushchev, the new leader of the USSR, gave a secret speech in 1956 in which he criticised Stalin's brutality. Consequently, Hungarians hoped for more freedom.
- ☑ Living standards had fallen and people were suffering.

 ### What happened during the Hungarian Uprising?

There were 4 key events during the Hungarian Uprising:

- ☑ In July 1956, people began to protest about the repressive nature of the government and low standards of living.
- ☑ Rakosi was replaced by Gero as prime minister in the hope protests would decrease.
- ☑ In October 1956 there were huge protests by students and workers demanding more freedom which turned into riots
- ☑ On 24th October, Nagy was appointed prime minister. He was more liberal and brought in reforms.

 ### What reforms did Nagy want to introduce during the Hungarian Uprising?

Nagy announced 5 key reforms, including:

- ☑ Relaxing censorship.
- ☑ Allowing free elections.
- ☑ Allowing non-communists into the government.
- ☑ A proposal for Hungary to withdraw from the Warsaw Pact *(p.41)*.
- ☑ The release of political prisoners, including Cardinal Jozsef Mindszenty who had been imprisoned by Rakosi.

 ### Why did the USSR invade Hungary during the Hungarian Uprising?

The USSR invaded Hungary because of Nagy's reforms and specifically because Nagy proposed that Hungary withdraw from the Warsaw Pact *(p.41)*.

 ### What happened as a consequence of the Hungarian Uprising?

There were 9 important consequences of the Hungarian Uprising:

- ☑ On 4th November, 1956, Khrushchev and the politburo ordered Soviet forces to invade Hungary with 200,000 troops to remove Nagy and crush the uprising.

- Between 20,000 and 30,000 Hungarians were killed.
- 1,000 Soviet troops died.
- 200,000 Hungarians became refugees.
- Nagy's government was deported, and Nagy was executed.
- Nagy was replaced by Janos Kadar and a new pro-Communist government loyal to the USSR was set up.
- All Nagy's reforms were reversed.
- This was used as a warning to other dissenting (protesting) countries in eastern Europe.
- It increased tension between the West and the East.

What was the response of the West to the Hungarian Uprising?

The West responded in 4 key ways:

- The United Nations condemned the Soviet actions.
- Spain, the Netherlands and Switzerland boycotted the 1956 Olympics.
- America accepted 80,000 refugees from Hungary.
- The USA could not send troops to help Hungary because the Warsaw Pact *(p.41)* would see it as an invasion and war would break out.

What did the new government do after the Hungarian Uprising?

The new Hungarian government, under Janos Kadar, remained under Soviet control and reacted in 3 key ways:

- It stamped out remaining resistance. 35,000 Hungarian protesters were arrested and 300 executed.
- A few of the reforms demanded by the Hungarians were introduced, cautiously.
- Kadar remained firmly in favour of Hungary's membership of the Warsaw Pact *(p.41)*.

What was the importance of the Hungarian Uprising?

The Hungarian Uprising was important because it affected the relationship between the USA and the USSR in 3 key ways:

- The USA supported the uprising but could not interfere, so now looked weak.
- Khrushchev's position was strengthened as a result.
- The USSR and the USA's relationship deteriorated because the USA had condemned the USSR's actions, increasing tension.

THE RED SCARE

'Now I am going to tell you how we are not going to fight communism. We are not going to transform our fine FBI into a Gestapo secret police. That is what some people would like to do.' - Harry Truman

What was the Second Red Scare?

After the Second World War, many people in America believed the communists were trying to take over America. It led to the Second Red Scare, with thousands of people put on trial and losing their jobs, often with very little proof.

When did the Second Red Scare happen?
The Second Red Scare was in the 1940s and 1950s.

What did the FBI do during the Second Red Scare?
The FBI, or Federal Bureau of Investigation, was anti-communist and played a big part in arresting those suspected of communism during the First Red Scare of 1919-20. As the Cold War began, they once again began collecting information on those they suspected of spying for the Soviet Union.

How many people did the Federal Loyalty Boards investigate during the second Red Scare?
3 million government employees were investigated between 1947 and 1951; approximately 3,000 were sacked or made to resign from their jobs.

What was the role of HUAC during the Second Red Scare?
HUAC, or the House Committee on Un-American Activities, had 2 main roles:

☑ It was created in 1938 to monitor any groups suspected of activities believed to be 'un-American'.

☑ From 1947, it began public hearings on the threat posed by the Communist Party of America. Suspected communists and witnesses were questioned and, depending on their responses, sent for trial.

What happened to the Hollywood Ten during the Second Red Scare?
The Hollywood Ten:

☑ Consisted of 10 Hollywood writers, producers and directors questioned by HUAC about communism within the film industry.

☑ Refused to answer any questions using the First Amendment of the US Constitution.

☑ Were jailed for one year and blacklisted from working in Hollywood.

What was the role of Alger Hiss during the Second Red Scare?
Alger Hiss was important during the Second Red Scare for 3 main reasons:

☑ He was a member of the state department who was accused of passing information to the Soviet Union.

☑ In 1949, he was put on trial and sentenced to 5 years in prison for lying to the court. Although he was never convicted of spying, many thought he must have been guilty of something.

☑ During the Hiss trial, the Soviet Union tested its first atomic bomb *(p. 18)*, heightening fears over communism.

What did the Rosenbergs do during the Second Red Scare?
The 4 key details of the Rosenberg case were:

☑ A married couple were accused of spying for the Soviet Union and passing secrets about the atomic bomb *(p. 18)*.

☑ They were found guilty in March 1951 and executed in June 1953.

☑ Some Americans thought the Rosenbergs were innocent, but many more believed they were responsible for helping the Soviet Union make its first atomic bomb *(p. 18)*.

☑ The case caused great fear in America, particularly as the couple's arrest coincided with the outbreak of the Korean War *(p. 36)*.

What did the McCarran Act do during the Second Red Scare?
The Second Red Scare had 2 main results:

☑ The McCarran Act was passed in August 1950, requiring all communist organisations to register with the government.

☑ The Act was strengthened in 1952, banning communists from holding US passports or having certain jobs.

What was McCarthy's role in the Second Red Scare?

Joseph McCarthy was a Republican senator. He conducted a powerful campaign against alleged communists which became known as the McCarthy witch hunts. He was widely believed at first, as Americans were worried about 'Reds under the bed', but his claims were later proven false.

> **DID YOU KNOW?**
>
> The science-fiction film, Invasion of the Body Snatchers, is often seen as a metaphor for McCarthyism.

THE U2 CRISIS

'We had absolutely failed to consider the 'what ifs' of the U-2 overflights in a thorough, realistic and searching manner. The shoot-down was a lesson that was burned into us by the way we mishandled it.' - Andrew Goodpaster, US Army General

What was the U2 Crisis?

The U2 Crisis happened when the Soviet Union shot down a U2 American spy plane.

What happened in the U2 Crisis?

The 4 key events in the story of the U2 Crisis are:

- ☑ US pilot Gary Powers flew a U2 spy plane over the Soviet Union to spy on its military capabilities.
- ☑ Khrushchev ordered the spy plane to be shot down and Powers was arrested and put on trial as a spy.
- ☑ The USA tried to claim it was only a weather plane, but the Soviets produced clear evidence it was a spy plane.
- ☑ Gary Powers was jailed for ten years by the Soviets.

When was the U2 crisis?

The U2 Crisis happened on 1st May, 1960.

What was the impact of the U2 crisis?

The U2 Crisis had 3 main consequences.

- ☑ Khrushchev stormed out of the Paris Peace Conference in 1960.
- ☑ The idea of the 'thaw' in tensions created during de-Stalinisation *(p.45)* was over. Tensions were now high again.
- ☑ President Kennedy *(p.66)* promised to be tougher on communism.

THE PARIS PEACE CONFERENCE, 1960

The Paris Peace Conference of 1960 was ruined by the U2 crisis, which wrecked the hopes for 'peaceful coexistence' between the superpowers.

What was the Paris Peace Conference in 1960?

The Paris Peace Conference (or Summit) of 1960 was intended to decrease tension between the two superpowers.

Why was there a Paris Peace Conference in 1960?

There were 2 reasons why the superpowers wanted a peace conference in 1960.

- ☑ As part of de-Stalinisation *(p.45)*, Khrushchev was pushing for 'peaceful coexistence' between capitalism and communism.
- ☑ Once McCarthyism and the 'Red Scare' was over, President Eisenhower felt he had the freedom to try to calm tensions in the Cold War, and to improve relations with the Soviet Union.

Who was at the 1960 Paris Peace Conference?

Nikita Khrushchev attended for the Soviet Union. President Dwight Eisenhower attended for the USA.

What happened at the Paris Peace Conference in 1960?

The Paris Peace Conference was a disaster: Khrushchev stormed out mid-way through, following the U2 Crisis *(p.49)*.

THE BERLIN WALL

The Berlin Wall is perhaps the number one symbol people think of when they imagine the Cold War - a physical wall, keeping capitalism and communism separate even in the same city.

What was the Berlin Wall?

The Berlin Wall, built by East Germany, divided East and West Berlin. It was constructed of concrete slabs in the city centre and barbed wire fences around the outer edges.

When was the Berlin Wall built?

The building of the Berlin Wall began on the 12th-13th August, 1961.

Why was the Berlin Wall built?

There were 2 main reasons for the building of the Berlin Wall:

- ☑ To prevent East German people defecting to West Berlin.
- ☑ To keep capitalism and spies from the West out, according to the Soviets and East German government.

What were the consequences of the Berlin Wall being built?

There were 7 key consequences of the building of the Berlin Wall:

- ☑ It solved the refugee crisis for East Germany, which now controlled who could leave and enter East Berlin.
- ☑ West Berlin remained under Allied control, making it harder for the Soviets to control the whole of East Germany.
- ☑ The number of military alerts in Berlin decreased as the situation there became less tense.

- It was a humiliation for the USSR and a propaganda victory for the West, as it appeared a wall was needed to prevent people fleeing.
- It divided West Berliners from East Berliners. Families and friends were separated for years.
- At least 140 people died attempting to cross the Berlin Wall from the east to the west between 1961 and 1989; some reports say the figure was higher.
- It became an iconic symbol of the Cold War.

What was President Kennedy's response to the building of the Berlin Wall?

President Kennedy's *(p.66)* responded in 2 main ways:

- He said: 'It's not a very nice solution but a wall is a hell of a lot better than a war.'.
- He visited West Berlin in June 1963, where he gave the 'Ich bin ein Berliner' speech to show his support for West Berliners.

What was the impact of the Berlin Wall on the relationship between the USA and the USSR?

There were both positive and negative effects on the relationship between the USA and the USSR:

- It solved the crisis over Berlin so reduced tension.
- There were fewer military alerts in Berlin as the situation had stabilised.
- Germany had been a source of conflict between the USSR and the USA since 1945. Their relationship had deteriorated so much a wall had to be built.
- It created a long-lasting symbol of the Cold War which signified the divide between the two sides.
- Khrushchev had suffered a humiliating defeat so decided to place missiles in Cuba to show he could stand up to the USA.
- Khrushchev saw Kennedy *(p.66)* as weak as he had not stopped the wall from being built.

What happened at Checkpoint Charlie after the Berlin Wall was built?

Two main points should be noted about what happened at Checkpoint Charlie:

- There was an 18-hour standoff when Soviet tanks stopped Americans crossing the border on 27th-28th October, 1961.
- It was a high point of tension between East and West until an agreement between the USA and USSR ended the incident.

DID YOU KNOW?

A trapeze artist called Horst Klein managed to escape over the Berlin Wall by tightrope walking across a power line in 1962. He fell and broke both his arms, but landed in West Berlin.

THE CUBAN REVOLUTION

'A revolution is not a bed of roses. A revolution is a struggle to the death between the future and the past.' - Fidel Castro, on the second anniversary of the Cuban Revolution.

What was the Cuban Revolution?

Fidel Castro led an armed uprising to bring down the dictatorship of the Cuban president, General Fulgencio Batista.

When was the Cuban Revolution?

The Cuban Revolution started in July 1953. Batista was removed from power on 31st December, 1958.

 Who started the Cuban Revolution?

Fidel Castro started the Cuban Revolution.

 How did the Cuban Revolution affect Cuba's relationship with the USA?

Before 1959, the USA supported Batista and there was co-operation between the two countries. This ended when diplomatic relations were broken off in January 1961.

 What was the USA's reaction to the Cuban Revolution?

The USA reacted in 7 key ways:

- ☑ It wanted Cuba back inside America's sphere of influence.
- ☑ In 1959, it refused to accept compensation offered by Cuba for American-owned property and land taken in the revolution.
- ☑ Although America did recognise Castro's government, when he requested economic aid in 1960 this was denied. Instead, President Eisenhower reduced US imports of Cuban sugar by 95%.
- ☑ It supported Cuban exiles to undermine the new government.
- ☑ It refused to buy Cuban sugar, which made up a large part of the national income, and eventually ended all trade with Cuba in October 1960.
- ☑ The CIA tried unsuccessfully to assassinate Castro.
- ☑ The CIA convinced President Kennedy *(p.66)* that the USA needed to invade Cuba.

 What became of Cuba's relationship with the USSR after the Cuban Revolution?

There were 3 important developments in Cuba's relationship with the Soviet Union:

- ☑ Cuba began to build economic links with the Soviet Union instead of the USA.
- ☑ In February 1960, it began to trade Cuban sugar for Soviet oil.
- ☑ Cuba wanted the Soviets' military defence and support.

DID YOU KNOW?

The Communist Party still rules in Cuba today.

THE BAY OF PIGS

The Bay of Pigs was one of the most catastrophic foreign policy interventions in American history.

 What happened at the Bay of Pigs in Cuba?

The Bay of Pigs incident involved Cuban exiles, supported by US forces, invading Cuba.

 When was the attack at the Bay of Pigs?

The invasion of Cuba at the Bay of Pigs took place on 17th April, 1961.

Who led the attack at the Bay of Pigs?

Cuban exiles, trained and supported by America, invaded Cuba at the Bay of Pigs.

What happened during the invasion of the Bay of Pigs?

There were 4 key events during the invasion of the Bay of Pigs:

- Castro learned about the invasion in advance because the planes were recognised as American from photographs.
- The 1,400 US-backed Cuban exiles were met by an army of 20,000 Cubans.
- The US-backed Cuban exiles surrendered.
- Almost all of those in the Cuban exile army were jailed or shot.

What were the consequences of the attack at the Bay of Pigs?

There were 5 important consequences of the attack at the Bay of Pigs:

- The incident meant USA-Cuban relations deteriorated while Soviet-Cuban relations improved.
- Fidel Castro stayed in power.
- The USA was totally discredited because it had supported illegal acts. President Kennedy *(p.66)* was embarrassed and his position was weakened.
- In December 1961, Castro stated he and his government were communist.
- Castro asked Khrushchev for military support in case of future attacks by the USA.

Why did the invasion at the Bay of Pigs fail?

There were 2 main reasons why the invasion at the Bay of Pigs failed:

- The CIA underestimated the strength of the Cubans, who had 20,000 troops and modern tanks and weapons.
- They also failed to gain the support of the Cuban people, which they assumed they would get.

DID YOU KNOW?

The failure of the Bay of Pigs invasion had several consequences.

President Kennedy was humiliated, and there were a number of failed attempts by the CIA to assassinate Fidel Castro.

THE CUBAN MISSILE CRISIS

The Cuban Missile crisis is often seen as the closest the human race has ever come to self-annihilation, as both superpowers were ready to resort to a potential nuclear war.

What was the Cuban Missile Crisis?

The Cuban Missile Crisis, between the USSR and the USA, was one of the most serious Cold War crises. It happened because the USSR placed missiles in Cuba and was the closest the world had been to a possible nuclear war.

When did the Cuban Missile Crisis happen?

The Cuban Missile Crisis lasted for 13 days, from 14th to 28th October, 1962.

Why did the Cuban Missile Crisis happen?

6 important causes of the Cuban Missile Crisis were:

- ☑ The long-term deterioration of the relationship between the USA and Cuba, accelerated by the Cuban Revolution *(p.51)* in 1959 and the Bay of Pigs incident in 1961.
- ☑ This pushed Cuba closer to the USSR, which bought Cuban sugar. In return, the Cubans bought oil from the Soviets.
- ☑ Castro had declared himself a Marxist in December 1961.
- ☑ Khrushchev was concerned about the missile gap and the fact the USA had nuclear missiles based in Turkey which could easily reach the USSR.
- ☑ The immediate cause was the deployment of Soviet nuclear missiles to Cuba for protection against possible attack by the USA.
- ☑ Cuba is only 160km south of the US state of Florida, which meant the mainland was within range of any missiles placed on Cuba. The USA therefore felt threatened.

What happened during the Cuban Missile Crisis?

There were 9 key events during the crisis in October 1962:

- ☑ On 14th October, American spy planes spotted missile bases being built on Cuba.
- ☑ On 16th October, Kennedy *(p.66)* was informed of the missile build-up and Ex-Comm, an advisory group, was formed.
- ☑ On 20th October, Kennedy *(p.66)* decided to blockade Cuba. This was a 500-mile naval 'quarantine' with the aim of preventing the Soviets bringing in further military supplies or missiles.
- ☑ On 24th October, Khrushchev stated the USSR would launch nuclear missiles if America went to war in Cuba.
- ☑ The blockade began. When Soviet ships approached the blockade, some stopped and some turned around.
- ☑ On 26th October, Kennedy *(p.66)* received a letter from Khrushchev who offered to negotiate if the blockade was removed and the USA did not invade Cuba.
- ☑ On 27th October, Kennedy *(p.66)* received a second letter from Khrushchev which offered to remove the missiles if the USA removed its missiles in Turkey.
- ☑ Kennedy's *(p.66)* brother, Robert, negotiated with the Russian ambassador and accepted the offer on condition the removal of missiles from Turkey was kept secret.
- ☑ On 28th October, Khrushchev agreed to the dismantling of the nuclear missiles.

How was the Cuban Missile Crisis solved?

The Cuban Missile Crisis was solved because:

- ☑ Khrushchev agreed to remove missiles from Cuba if the USA removed its warheads from Italy and Turkey.
- ☑ The USA would only agree to the deal if the removal of its missiles from Italy and Turkey was kept secret.

What were the results of the Cuban Missile Crisis?

There were 6 main consequences to the Cuban Missile Crisis:

- ☑ Cuba survived as a communist country.
- ☑ Kennedy *(p.66)* assured the world that the USA would never invade Cuba and his public image improved.
- ☑ The Soviet Union looked weak because the world did not know the USA had removed its missiles from Turkey.
- ☑ Khrushchev lost power in the USSR and was dismissed in 1964.
- ☑ China criticised the USSR over its actions because the Soviets had made the communist world look weak. China's relationship with the USSR deteriorated.
- ☑ The USA's NATO *(p.40)* allies in Europe were horrified because they had not been consulted. France reacted by leaving NATO in 1966.

Quizzes, amazing exam preparation tools and more at GCSEHistory.com

How did the Cuban Missile Crisis affect the relationship between the USA and the USSR?

The Cuban Missile Crisis had 2 main effects on the relationship between the USA and the USSR:

- The relationship had deteriorated almost to the brink of nuclear war, so Kennedy (p.66) wanted to focus more on the two nations' 'common interests'.
- A hotline was set up in June 1963 between the USA and the USSR. This would help avoid crises by enabling direct and quick communication.

Why was the Cuban Missile Crisis important?

The Cuban Missile Crisis was important for 2 main reasons:

- It was the most dangerous Cold War confrontation between the USA and the USSR and almost led to nuclear war.
- It resulted in both countries working to improve their relationship and slow down the arms race.

What nuclear treaties were signed after The Cuban Missile Crisis?

There were 3 important nuclear treaties signed after the Cuban Missile Crisis:

- 1963 - the Limited Test Ban Treaty banned the testing of nuclear weapons in air or underwater.
- 1967 - the Outer Space Treaty banned testing or using nuclear weapons in space.
- 1968 - the Nuclear Non-Proliferation Treaty stated the ultimate goal was world nuclear disarmament.

DID YOU KNOW?

One man, Vasili Arkhipov, is credited with 'saving the world' by refusing to fire nuclear missiles during the crisis. His actions may have prevented an all out nuclear war.

THE PRAGUE SPRING, 1968

'I have worked for thirty years in the Party, and my whole family has devoted everything to the affairs of the Party, the affairs of socialism. Let whatever is going to happen to me happen. I'm expecting the worst for myself and I'm resigned to it.' - Alexander Dubček, in a discussion with Brezhnev in 1968.

What was the Prague Spring?

The Prague Spring is the term used for the brief period when the government of Czechoslovakia wanted to democratise the nation and reduce the control the USSR had on the country.

When was the Prague Spring?

The Prague Spring took place between 5th January and 21st August in 1968.

Who was responsible for the Prague Spring?

Alexander Dubček, the new leader of Czechoslovakia, introduced the reforms.

What were the causes of the Prague Spring?

There were 6 main reasons for the Prague Spring.

- Since 1957, Czechoslovakia had been led by Antonin Novotný, who was very unpopular because he was a hard-line communist.
- Novotný did not bring in reforms, despite Khrushchev's de-Stalinisation *(p.45)* policy.
- By the 1960s, the Czech economy was struggling, and the standard of living was decreasing.
- When the leader of the USSR, Brezhnev, visited Czechoslovakia in December 1967, he withdrew his support for Novotný because he was so unpopular.
- Novotný was replaced by Dubček as the leader of Czechoslovakia on 5th January, 1968, in the hope that this would reduce discontent.
- Dubček wanted to reform communism to create 'socialism with a human face'. This would enable the public to be more involved in the government and, hopefully, increase support for communism.

What were the reforms of the Prague Spring introduced by Dubček?

Dubček brought in 7 main reforms.

- Censorship was relaxed in April 1968, which allowed more criticism of communism.
- Free speech was allowed.
- Political parties other than the Communist Party were allowed to exist.
- Work councils were set up to represent workers and improve working conditions.
- The secret police had their powers restricted, so their ability to arrest and detain people without trial was reduced.
- Some capitalist elements were even allowed, to create a form of 'market socialism' economy.
- Travel restrictions were lifted, so Czechs could travel abroad.

What was the response from the Czechoslovakian Communist Party to the Prague Spring?

The response from the leaders of the Czechoslovakian Communist Party was not enthusiastic.

- Many were horrified at Dubček's reforms, believing they were a threat to communism.
- On 3rd August, 1968, 5 leading opponents of the Prague Spring reforms sent a letter to Brezhnev, outlining their concerns and asking him to intervene.

Why were Eastern Bloc leaders concerned during the Prague Spring?

Brezhnev, the leader of the USSR, and Erich Honecker, the leader of East Germany, were very worried for 3 main reasons.

- Romania would not attend Warsaw Pact *(p.41)* meetings.
- Tito, the leader of Yugoslavia, did not want the USSR to control his country.
- They feared the Prague Spring would lead to calls for reform elsewhere in the Soviet Union's sphere of influence.

What was Brezhnev's response to the Prague Spring?

Brezhnev and the Eastern Bloc responded in 12 main ways.

- In July 1968, the USSR claimed to know of plans by West Germany to invade the Sudetenland, and asked to send Soviet troops to protect Czechoslovakia. Dubček refused.
- The USSR considered economic sanctions for Czechoslovakia, but didn't want the country to seek help from the West.
- In July, the entire Soviet Politburo (cabinet) visited Czechoslovakia, to put pressure on Dubček to reverse the reforms
- Warsaw Pact *(p.41)* troops from the USSR, Poland and East Germany completed manoeuvres in Czechoslovakia in the summer, to put more pressure on Dubček.
- On 15th July, members of the Warsaw Pact *(p.41)* sent a letter to Dubček, warning him that the reforms were dangerous to the Eastern Bloc.
- On 20th-21st August, 1968, 500,000 Soviet-led Warsaw Pact *(p.41)* troops entered Prague to arrest the reformers.

- Nobody in Czechoslovakia was expecting an invasion, especially their armed troops, who were completely unprepared.
- Dubček and other leaders were arrested. They were taken to Moscow to meet Brezhnev.
- Dubček was forced to sign the Moscow Protocol, which stated that Czechoslovakia would protect communism and the reforms would be reversed.
- All the reforms were reversed when Dubček returned to Czechoslovakia.
- In August 1968, the Brezhnev Doctrine (p.58) was created. The USSR had the right to invade any country in its sphere of influence which threatened the stability of eastern Europe.
- The USSR wanted to ensure it had full control over Czechoslovakia. In 1969, therefore, it replaced Dubček with Husak, a hard-line and reliable communist.

What was the reaction of the West to the Prague Spring and the Soviet invasion?

The West reacted in 3 key ways.

- The UN wanted to condemn the invasion of Czechoslovakia by Warsaw Pact (p.41) troops, but the USSR vetoed it.
- The USA and the West condemned the invasion.
- However, the USA did nothing because it was distracted by Vietnam, there was a US presidential election, and it was the beginning of détente.

What was the reaction of the communist world to the Prague Spring and the Soviet invasion?

The communist world reacted in 5 main ways.

- Communists in western countries condemned the invasion, and created their own version of communism called Eurocommunism.
- In France and Italy, the Communist Party condemned the USSR's actions.
- Yugoslavia and Romania spoke out against the USSR's invasion, which worsened their relationship with the Soviet Union.
- Poland and East Germany were very supportive of the invasion, as they were trying to control reformers in their own countries.
- Communist China (p.35) condemned the USSR invasion of Czechoslovakia, and the relationship between the two countries greatly deteriorated.

What was the importance of the Prague Spring?

The Prague Spring and the invasion by Soviet troops were important for 3 key reasons.

- They led to the creation of the Brezhnev Doctrine (p.58), which increased USSR control over eastern Europe.
- It split the communist world, as communist parties in western Europe became independent of the USSR's control, and communist China (p.35) condemned the invasion.
- It highlighted that, while the USA would condemn the USSR's actions, it wouldn't take any steps to stop them.

DID YOU KNOW?

137 Czechoslovaks were killed resisting the Soviet invasion.

THE BREZHNEV DOCTRINE

'When forces that are hostile to socialism try to turn the development of some socialist country towards capitalism, it becomes not only a problem of the country concerned, but a common problem and concern of all socialist countries.' - Leonid Brezhnev, 1968.

What was the Brezhnev Doctrine?

The Brezhnev Doctrine stated that the USSR had the right to invade any country in its sphere of influence which threatened the stability of eastern Europe.

Who was behind the Brezhnev Doctrine?

Leonid Brezhnev, the leader of the USSR between 1964 and 1982, created the Brezhnev Doctrine.

Why was the Brezhnev Doctrine introduced?

Brezhnev introduced the Brezhnev Doctrine after the Prague Spring *(p. 55)* because he realised he could not allow reforms in other eastern European nations.

When was the Brezhnev Doctrine created?

The Brezhnev Doctrine was created in September 1968.

How did the West react to the Brezhnev Doctrine?

The West reacted to the Brezhnev Doctrine in 3 main ways:

- ☑ It was condemned by the USA.
- ☑ Communist parties in the democratic west were shocked and broke away from the Soviet Communist Party to create their own version of communism, called Eurocommunism.
- ☑ It was condemned by the UN.

How did the communists react to the Brezhnev Doctrine?

Other communist states reacted in the 3 main ways to the Brezhnev Doctrine:

- ☑ Communist governments in East Germany and Poland welcomed it because they were attempting to control reformers in their own countries.
- ☑ Romania and Yugoslavia were horrified and tried to distance themselves from the USSR and be more independent.
- ☑ China was angered and insulted by the Brezhnev Doctrine, as it only gave the USSR the right to intervene. Their relationship deteriorated.

What was the significance of the Brezhnev Doctrine for eastern Europe?

Countries in the eastern European bloc now had to obey strict Soviet rule or risk invasion.

ONGOING TENSION

Although both superpowers had seen the danger of continued hostility following the Cuban Missile Crisis, a few factors made it difficult for a full reconciliation.

 ### What tensions were there during detente?

Despite improved relations between the superpowers during the period of detente, they were still distrustful of each other. Two areas in particular still caused tension: America's role in Vietnam, and the Soviet Union's record on human rights.

 ### What tension was there over Vietnam in the detente period?

American involvement in Vietnam limited cooperation during detente for both superpowers in 2 main ways.

- ☑ It was difficult for the Soviets to trust the USA, when the USA was prepared to crush communism in countries that had adopted it freely.
- ☑ It was difficult for American government to justify a closer relationship with the USSR to the American public, when they were pouring men and equipment into Vietnam to defeat the communist threat.

What tension was there over human rights in the detente period?

Human rights in the USSR remained an area of tension between the superpowers in 3 main ways.

- ☑ Western leaders contrasted perceived Soviet oppression with Western freedoms, while the Soviets viewed this attitude as political interference in a domestic matter.
- ☑ Under Brezhnev there was a crackdown on individual freedoms, including censorship of the press and imprisonment for political critics.
- ☑ A crackdown on human rights was also evident outside the USSR, in areas of Soviet control: for example, the Prague Spring *(p.55)* n 1968.

DÉTENTE

'One has to be broad-minded and tolerant enough to understand the possibility and the desirability of coexistence and cooperation between nations that are vastly different in their social systems, political institutions, values, sympathies and antipathies.' - Georgi Arbatov, Soviet Central committee member, 1983.

 ### What was détente?

Détente refers to a period during the Cold War where tensions between the USA and the Soviet Union were eased. There was increased cooperation and several attempts were made to slow down the arms race.

 ### When did détente happen?

Détente was between 1967 and 1979.

 ### What role did Henry Kissinger play in détente?

Henry Kissinger was very important to détente in 3 key ways:

- ☑ As President Nixon's security advisor, he organised Nixon's trips to Moscow and China in 1972.
- ☑ He also played an important role in the SALT 1 *(p.61)* talks.
- ☑ As Secretary of State, Kissinger helped end the Vietnam War *(p.38)* for which he jointly received the Nobel Peace Prize in 1973.

Why was the policy of détente introduced?

Détente occurred for 7 key reasons:

- Both the USSR and the USA wanted to ease tensions after the Cuban Missile Crisis *(p.53)* because they came so close to nuclear war.
- The Sino-Soviet relationship had deteriorated and the USSR wanted to prevent the USA becoming closer to China. The Soviets were worried when President Nixon visited China in 1972.
- Brezhnev, the leader of the USSR, wanted an improved relationship with the USA as he wanted access to US technology and grain.
- Both sides wanted to slow down the arms race because it was very expensive and they needed the money for domestic issues.
- The USA had domestic problems with anti-Vietnam War *(p.38)* demonstrations, race riots and massive social inequality. It needed to cut defence spending so it could invest at home.
- The USSR had economic problems and needed to cut defence spending so there was money to invest at home.
- The USA needed the USSR's help to end the Vietnam War *(p.38)* as they were supplying the Vietnamese communists. To find a solution, the USA asked the USSR for help.

What were the key events of détente?

The 9 key events of détente were:

- 1968: Nuclear Non-Proliferation Treaty.
- 1970: Relations between East Germany and West Germany improved with the policy of Ostpolitik.
- 1970: Ostpolitik resulted in the Treaty of Warsaw, which recognised the existing borders between the countries.
- 1972: SALT 1 *(p.61)*.
- 1972: President Nixon visited China to meet Chairman Mao and visited Brezhnev in Moscow.
- 1972: Ostpolitik continued with the signing of the Basic Treaty which established formal relations between the two German nations.
- 1973: Brezhnev, leader of the USSR, visited Washington to meet Nixon.
- 1975: Helsinki Accords and the Apollo-Soyuz Missions.
- 1979: SALT 2.

What role did Ostpolitik play in détente?

Ostpolitik was the policy of Chancellor Willy Brandt of West Germany which aimed to reduce tensions between the two German nations.

What was the importance of détente?

The move towards détente led to the signing of the Strategic Arms Limitation Treaties, or SALT. These treaties were intended to limit the arms race in strategic ballistic missiles armed with nuclear weapons.

Why did détente end?

The main reason détente ended was due to the USSR's invasion of Afghanistan in December 1979.

> **DID YOU KNOW?**
>
> The word 'détente' is French and means 'easing of tension.'

SALT 1

The Strategic Arms Limitation Talks were the first concrete steps taken to control and reduce the arms race.

What was SALT 1?

The Strategic Arms Limitation Treaty, or SALT 1, was an agreement between the superpowers to limit their number of nuclear weapons.

When was SALT 1 signed?

SALT 1 was signed on 26th May, 1972.

Who signed SALT 1?

The SALT 1 agreement was signed between Richard Nixon and Leonid Brezhnev.

What was agreed in SALT 1?

There were 4 important agreements in SALT 1:

- [x] The Anti-Ballistic Missile Treaty: anti-ballistic missiles (ABMs) were allowed at only two sites, with 100 missiles at each.
- [x] The Interim Treaty: limited the number of intercontinental ballistic missiles (ICBMs) and submarine launched cruise missiles (SLBMs) the USA and USSR could have. The USA was allowed 1054 ICBMs, and the USSR 1618.
- [x] There would be a five-year delay in building more missiles, so another treaty (SALT 2) would have to be negotiated at the end of that time.
- [x] The Basic Principles Agreement: established what the USA and USSR would do to avoid nuclear war breaking out and the rules if it did occur.

What were the limitations of SALT 1?

SALT 1 was limited in 3 main ways because:

- [x] It did not cover intermediate-range nuclear weapons, which were still being deployed by both countries.
- [x] It did not include multiple independently targeted reentry vehicles (MIRVs) which carried multiple warheads on a single missile.
- [x] Although it slowed down the arms race, both sides still had enough nuclear missiles to destroy the planet and there was no agreement to not use those missiles.

Why was SALT 1 important?

SALT 1 was important because of 3 key reasons:

- [x] It slowed the arms race.
- [x] It showed an improvement in relations between the USA and the Soviet Union.
- [x] It led to further improvements such as the Helsinki Conference in 1975 and the SALT 2 negotiations.

PRIME MINISTER ATTLEE

Clement Attlee was the Prime Minister of Britain from 1945 to 1951.

Who was Clement Attlee?

Clement Attlee was a Labour politician who served as prime minister of the United Kingdom from 1945 to 1951.

What were Clement Attlee's beliefs?

Attlee had left-wing beliefs and his government is most famous for creating the NHS. Attlee supported the Marshall Plan *(p.30)* and promoted a NATO *(p.40)* military alliance against the USSR and its satellite states.

What conferences did Clement Attlee attend?

Attlee attended the Potsdam Conference *(p.20)* in July 1945, to discuss Nazi Germany and how to end the war.

DID YOU KNOW?

Attlee trained as a lawyer, fought in the First World War and was the founding father of the NHS.

FULGENCIO BATISTA

Fulgencio Batista was nicknamed 'El Hombre' or 'the man'.

Who was Batista?

Fulgencio Batista was the American-backed dictator of Cuba from 1952 to 1959, until he was overthrown by Fidel Castro in the Cuban Revolution *(p.51)*.

LEONID BREZHNEV

Leonid Brezhnev was the fourth leader of the USSR.

Who was Leonid Brezhnev?

Leonid Brezhnev was the fifth leader of the Soviet Union from 1964 until his death in 1982.

What was the doctrine Brezhnev used?

The Brezhnev Doctrine *(p.58)* was established in 1968. This stated that the actions of an individual communist country affected all communist countries, therefore others must take action to ensure the survival of the regime.

What was Brezhnev's reaction to Reagan's Zero Option proposal?

Brezhnev rejected President Reagan's Zero Option proposal in November 1981, in which Reagan offered to cancel the deployment of intermediate-range missiles in Europe if the USSR dismantled theirs.

PRIME MINISTER CHURCHILL

Prime Minister Churchill led Britain during the Second World War.

Who was Winston Churchill?

Sir Winston Churchill was Prime Minister of the United Kingdom from 1940 to 1945, and again from 1951 to 1955.

What were Churchill's beliefs?

Churchill was a conservative with traditional values. He strongly valued democracy, was in favour of empire, and was incredibly suspicious of Stalin.

What was Churchill's views on the policy of appeasement?

Winston Churchill was an opponent of appeasement, describing it as 'an unmitigated disaster'. Churchill told Britain and France they would have to choose between war and dishonour, and that Hitler was not done expanding the Third Reich.

ALEXANDER DUBČEK

Dubček was the rebel leader of communist Czechoslovakia.

Who was Dubček?

Alexander Dubček was a leader of Czechoslovakia. He had a good relationship with Soviet leader Leonid Brezhnev, supported the Warsaw Pact *(p.41)* and wanted to introduce reforms to improve people's lives.

When was Dubček in power?

Alexander Dubček was the leader of Czechoslovakia from January 1968 to August 1968.

What were Dubček reforms called?

Dubček introduced reforms known as the Prague Spring *(p.55)* to create 'socialism with a human face'.

What reforms did Dubček introduce?

There were 4 main reforms introduced by Dubček:

- He relaxed censorship.
- Other political parties were also permitted.
- The secret police had their powers reduced.
- Some capitalist elements were even allowed to create a form of "market socialism" economy.

What happened to Dubček afterwards?

The following happened to Dubček:

- Dubček was arrested and forced to visit Moscow.
- He was ordered to reverse all his reforms.
- In 1969, Dubček was replaced by Husak, who was a hardline communist Moscow could rely on.
- He was appointed Ambassador to Turkey until he was expelled from the party, and then he worked in forest administration.

DID YOU KNOW?

Dubček believed Lenin (the first leader of the Soviet Union) had been wrong about some things, and allowing some elements of capitalism was necessary.

PRESIDENT EISENHOWER

There were key events in the Cold War when President Eisenhower was in power: the Korean War, the Warsaw Pact was created, Khrushchev gave his 'Secret Speech' and the U2 spy plane incident were just some of them.

Who was President Eisenhower?

Dwight D Eisenhower was the 34th President of the United States.

When was Eisenhower president?

Eisenhower was President of the United States from 1953 until 1961.

 What was President Eisenhower's background?

President Eisenhower's background included the following:

- Eisenhower was a member of the US armed forces throughout the 1920s and 1930s.
- He was a general in the army during the Second World War and was in charge of the D-Day landings in 1944.
- He became the supreme commander of NATO *(p.40)* in December 1950.
- His war record helped him secure the presidency.

 What were the key events of Eisenhower's presidency?

Some of the key events of Eisenhower's presidency included:

- In 1953 he helped negotiate an armistice that brought peace to Korea.
- He committed the USA to protecting South Vietnam from communism in 1953.

- He was in power during the Montgomery Bus Boycott, led by Rosa Parks, which lasted for twelve months between 1955 and 1956.
- In 1957 he signed the Civil Rights Act and set up a permanent Civil Rights Commission.

What were Eisenhower's beliefs about the Cold War?

Eisenhower was anti-communist and committed to the policy of containment. He articulated the concept of the 'Domino Theory'.

What uprising was Eisenhower involved in?

Eisenhower managed to increase tensions between the East and the West when he refused to send US troops to help the Hungarian Uprisings. This led to Eastern Bloc countries realising the West would not support them.

Did Eisenhower send a spy to the USSR?

In 1960, Khrushchev walked out of a meeting after Eisenhower refused to apologise for sending a U2 spy plane to spy on the Soviet Union.

What actions did Eisenhower take on civil rights?

Eisenhower took 3 key actions related to civil rights:

- He introduced the Civil Rights Act of 1957 that sought to ensure all African Americans could register to vote.
- Following the ruling in the case of Brown v Board of Education, Eisenhower did not want to use his powers to support the rapid desegregation of schools as he believed it should proceed slowly.
- He sent federal troops to Little Rock to protect the African American students and enforce integration.

DID YOU KNOW?

President Eisenhower gave a speech after Stalin died called 'Chance for Peace.'

In that speech, he calls on the USSR work for peace.

GEORGE KENNAN

George F. Kennan was a historian and a diplomat.

Who was George Kennan?

George Kennan was an American diplomat and the US ambassador in Moscow.

What were Kennan's beliefs?

Kennan was a strong advocate of the US policy of containment and was suspicious of the Soviet Union.

What telegram did Kennan send?

In 1946, Kennan sent the 'Long Telegram *(p.21)*' to Truman. This reported hostile attitudes in Moscow towards the USA and said Stalin wanted to destroy capitalism.

PRESIDENT JOHN F KENNEDY

'I take pride in the words Ich bin ein Berliner.' - President Kennedy on visiting Berlin

Who was President Kennedy?

John F Kennedy, commonly referred to as JFK, was the 35th President of the United States.

When was Kennedy president?

John F Kennedy was president between January 1961 and November 1963.

What was Kennedy's background?

Kennedy's background included the following:

- ☑ He came from an Irish-American family which was very wealthy and heavily involved in politics.
- ☑ He went to Harvard University and studied politics. He wrote his dissertation on Britain's policy of the appeasement of Adolf Hitler.
- ☑ He was in the US navy and served in the Second World War, where he was seriously injured when his boat was destroyed by the Japanese.

What were the key events of Kennedy's presidency?

The key events of Kennedy's presidency included the following:

- ☑ Kennedy created the Peace Corps in 1961.
- ☑ The Bay of Pigs Invasion in Cuba, in April 1961.
- ☑ In May 1961 he pledged America would put a man on the moon by the end of the decade.
- ☑ The Berlin Wall *(p.50)* was built in 1961.
- ☑ The Cuban Missile Crisis *(p.53)* took place in October 1962.
- ☑ He signed the Limited Nuclear Test Ban Treaty in August 1963.

What were Kennedy's beliefs about the Cold War?

Kennedy was anti-communist and, like his predecessors, was committed to containing communism. However, he was aware of the dangers of nuclear warfare after tensions were brought to the brink during the Cuban Missile Crisis *(p.53)*, and wanted to reduce the chances of nuclear war.

What was President Kennedy's role in the Bay of Pigs invasion?

Kennedy attempted to implement a counter-revolution in Cuba by sending in Cuban exiles. The aim was to make it look like the USA wasn't involved. However, the plan failed.

What was President Kennedy's involvement with the Cuban Missile Crisis?

In 1962, two U2 spy planes spotted what looked like missiles in Cuba. This led to a tense 13 days where Kennedy deliberated what to do. He decided to set up a naval blockade and managed to prevent nuclear war.

What was President Kennedy's role in Vietnam?

President Kennedy continued to support South Vietnam with money, military advisers and commandos.

How did President Kennedy die?

Kennedy was assassinated in November 1963 in Dallas, Texas.

Why was President Kennedy in Dallas?

Kennedy was in Dallas because he needed to win support from the southern Democrats, nicknamed the Dixiecrats, for his Civil Rights bill.

NIKITA KHRUSHCHEV

Nikita Khrushchev was third leader of the USSR.

Who was Khrushchev?

Nikita Khrushchev led the Soviet Union after Stalin's death up until 1964.

What was Khrushchev's speech?

Khrushchev openly criticised Stalin in his 'Secret Speech' in 1956. Khrushchev began to de-Stalinise the Soviet Union and said he wanted a peaceful co-existence with the West. People hoped this would end the Cold War.

How did tensions increase under Khrushchev?

The Hungarian Uprising *(p.46)* managed to increase international tensions as countries in eastern Europe began to realise the USA would not help them.

DID YOU KNOW?

Khrushchev was the son of a peasant from the Ukraine.

He was not well educated but rose through the ranks of the Communist Party. Despite his criticism of Stalin's brutality in his 'Secret Speech', he was involved in the Great Purges of the 1930s.

GEORGE MARSHALL

George C. Marshall had a long military career and was partly responsible for the Normandy invasion of 1944.

Who was Marshall?

George C Marshall was a general in the American army and statesman. He served as Secretary of State and Secretary of Defense under President Truman.

What plan did George Marshall come up with?

The Marshall Plan *(p.30)* aimed to provide economic aid to war-torn countries in Europe. The purpose of this was keep them tied to the USA instead of falling to communism.

DID YOU KNOW?

George C. Marshall was awarded the Nobel Peace Prize in 1953 for creating the Marshall Plan.

IMRE NAGY

Imre Nagy was a life-long member of the Communist Party.

Who was Imre Nagy?

Imre Nagy was a Hungarian communist politician who served as Prime Minister from 1953 to 1955 and again during the Hungarian Uprising *(p.46)* in 1956.

What uprising was Nagy involved in?

Nagy introduced reforms that Khrushchev accepted. However, Nagy then announced that Hungary was leaving the Warsaw Pact *(p.41)*, so Khrushchev sent in the Red Army.

How did Nagy die?

As a result of the Hungarian Uprising *(p.46)*, Nagy was executed.

DID YOU KNOW?

Nagy was executed by being hanged in 1958.

Quizzes, amazing exam preparation tools and more at GCSEHistory.com

NIKOLAI NOVIKOV

Nikolai Novikov's telegram greatly influenced Stalin's attitudes towards the USA.

 ## Who was Nikolai Novikov?

Nikolai Novikov was a Soviet diplomat and the USSR's ambassador in Washington.

What was Novikov's telegram?

Stalin received a telegram from Novikov which reported that America wanted to dominate the world and was preparing for war with the USSR.

ANTONIN NOVOTNÝ

Antonin Novotný was hard-line Stalinist.

 ## Who was Novotný?

Antonin Novotný was the communist Prime Minister of Czechoslovakia from 1957 to 1968.

What important events occurred while Novotný was leader?

Novotný was leader when the Prague Spring *(p.55)* began, where people tried to reform the communist system in Czechoslovakia to create 'socialism with a human face'.

DID YOU KNOW?

Novotný was allowed to re-join the Central Committee of the Czechoslovakian Communist Party after the Prague Spring but he never regained his power.

PRESIDENT ROOSEVELT

President Roosevelt played a key role in two of the three wartime meetings of the Grand Alliance.

What were President Roosevelt's beliefs during the Second World War?

President Roosevelt strongly believed in democracy. However, he formed an alliance with the USSR to protect the USA against Japan. He believed Stalin could be 'managed' and remain a post-war ally.

What conferences did Roosevelt attend at the end of the Second World War to discuss his ideas?

President Roosevelt attended the Tehran and Yalta conferences, which discussed Nazi Germany and how to end the war.

PRESIDENT TRUMAN

'I believe that it must be the policy of the United States to support free peoples who are resisting attempted subjugation by armed minorities or by outside pressures.' - President Truman, 1947.

Who was President Truman?

Harry S Truman was the 33rd President of the United States, holding office from 1945 to 1953.

What was an overview of Truman's time as president?

Truman's time as president included the following events:

- He took over from Franklin D Roosevelt during the Second World War.
- He oversaw huge challenges both domestically and internationally as America transitioned from fighting the Second World War in 1945 to the onset of the Cold War between 1947 and 1949.
- His policy of the Truman Doctrine *(p.29)* and the policy of the containment became the cornerstone of American foreign policy for decades.
- In the years after his presidency he faced huge criticism as the president who 'lost China to communism'.
- He is now considered by historians to be one of America's greatest presidents.

What was President Truman's attitude towards communism?

Truman objected to the USSR's control over the countries of eastern Europe. He believed the USSR was determined to expand, so he sought to contain the spread of communism during his time in office.

What conferences did Truman attend?

Truman attended the Potsdam Conference *(p.20)* in July 1945 to discuss Nazi Germany and how to end the war.

What was Truman's involvement in the Cold War?

The Truman Doctrine *(p.29)*, in 1947, highlighted America's new stance on communism, and signalled the beginning of the US policy of containment.

What actions did Truman take in support of civil rights?

President Truman took 2 main actions in support of civil rights:

- In 1946, he set up the 'President's Committee on Civil Rights', which aimed to abolish segregation.
- He ended segregation in the armed forces by issuing executive order 9981 on 26th July, 1948.

What was the impact of President Truman's civil rights policies?

There were 3 main results of President Truman's civil rights policies:

- White people in the southern states were horrified.
- In 1948, some members broke away from the Democrat Party to create the States' Rights Democratic Party, nicknamed the 'Dixiecrats'.
- It gained President Truman support from African Americans, which helped in the 1948 elections.

DID YOU KNOW?

Harry S Truman's middle name was, literally, 'S'.

It was included to honour his grandfathers, who both had 'S' in their names.

A

Abolish, Abolished - to stop something, or get rid of it.

Aggression - angry, hostile or violent behaviour displayed without provocation.

Agricultural - relating to agriculture.

Alliance - a union between groups or countries that benefits each member.

Allies - parties working together for a common objective, such as countries involved in a war. In both world wars, 'Allies' refers to those countries on the side of Great Britain.

Ambassador - someone, often a diplomat, who represents their state, country or organisation in a different setting or place.

Armistice - an agreement between two or more opposing sides in a war to stop fighting.

Artillery - large guns used in warfare.

Assassinate - to murder someone, usually an important figure, often for religious or political reasons.

B

Blacklist - the blocking of trade as a means to punish.

Blockade - a way of blocking or sealing an area to prevent goods, supplies or people from entering or leaving. It often refers to blocking transport routes.

Boycott - a way of protesting or bringing about change by refusing to buy something or use services.

Brinkmanship - pushing a disagreement to its limits in the hope the other side backs down, especially pertaining to war.

Buffer - a protective barrier.

Buffer zone - a neutral area of land to separate hostile forces or nations and provide protection. In the Cold War, Eastern Europe was the buffer zone between Western Europe and the USSR.

C

Cabinet - politically, the group of senior ministers responsible for controlling government policy.

Campaign - a political movement to get something changed; in military terms, it refers to a series of operations to achieve a goal.

Capitalism - the idea of goods and services being exchanged for money, private ownership of property and businesses, and acceptance of a hierarchical society.

Censorship - the control of information in the media by a government, whereby information considered obscene or unacceptable is suppressed.

Civil rights - the rights a citizen has to political or social freedoms, such as the right to vote or freedom of speech.

Coalition government - a government formed by more than one political party.

Coalition, Coalitions - a temporary alliance, such as when a group of countries fights together.

Coexistence - living or existing together at the same time or in the same place.

Collective security - a policy adopted by the League of Nations, with the idea members should feel safe from attack as all nations agreed to defend each other.

Colonies, Colony - a country or area controlled by another country and occupied by settlers.

Communism - the belief, based on the ideas of Karl Marx, that all people should be equal in society without government, money or private property. Everything is owned by by the people, and each person receives according to need.

Communist - a believer in communism.

Conference - a formal meeting to discuss common issues of interest or concern.

Conservative - someone who dislikes change and prefers traditional values. It can also refer to a member of the Conservative Party.

Constitution - rules, laws or principles that set out how a country is governed.

Containment - meaning to keep something under control or within limits, it often refers to the American idea of stopping the spread of communism.

Cooperate, Cooperation - to work together to achieve a common aim. Frequently used in relation to politics, economics or law.

Currency - an umbrella term for any form of legal tender, but most commonly referring to money.

D

Deadlock - a situation where no action can be taken and neither side can make progress against the other; effectively a draw.

Defect - the act of defection; to leave your country or cause for another.

Demilitarised - to remove all military forces from an area and forbid them to be stationed there.

Democracy - a political system where a population votes for its government on a regular basis. The word is Greek for 'the rule of people' or 'people power'.

Democratic - relating to or supporting the principles of democracy.

Deploy - to move military troops or equipment into position or a place so they are ready for action.

Deport - to expel someone from a country and, usually, return them to their homeland.

Desegregation - a policy of removing racial segregation (separation).

Deterrent - something that discourages an action or behaviour.

Dictator - a ruler with absolute power over a country, often acquired by force.

Dictatorship - a form of government where an individual or small group has total power, ruling without tolerance for other views or opposition.

Disarmament - the reduction or removal of weaponry.

Dispute - a disagreement or argument; often used to describe conflict between different countries.

Dissent, Dissenting - to hold or express views against an idea or policy, often in politics.

Doctrine - a stated principle of government policy; can also refer to a set of beliefs held and taught by a church, political party or other group.

Dollar imperialism - a phrase used by the Soviet Union's Foreign Minister, Molotov, in accusing the USA of using its economic strength to take over Europe through the Marshall Plan.

Détente - the easing of tension, especially between two countries.

E

Economic - relating to the economy; also used when justifying something in terms of profitability.

Economy - a country, state or region's position in terms of production and consumption of goods and services, and the supply of money.

Empire - a group of states or countries ruled over and controlled by a single monarch.

Exile - to be banned from one's original country, usually as a punishment or for political reasons.

F

Fascist - one who believes in fascism.

Federal - in US politics this means 'national', referring to the whole country rather than any individual state.

Foreign policy - a government's strategy for dealing with other nations.

Free elections - elections in which voters are free to vote without interference.

G

Guerrilla tactics, Guerrilla warfare - a way of fighting that typically involves hit-and-run style tactics.

Guerrillas - groups of small, independent fighters usually involved in a war against larger, regular military forces.

H

Hard line - strict and uncompromising.

I

Ideology - a set of ideas and ideals, particularly around political

ideas or economic policy, often shared by a group of people.

Imperial, Imperialisation, Imperialism, Imperialist - is the practice or policy of taking possession of, and extending political and economic control over other areas or territories. Imperialism always requires the use of military, political or economic power by a stronger nation over that of a weaker one. An imperialist is someone who supports or practices imperialism and imperial relates to a system of empire, for example the British Empire.

Import - to bring goods or services into a different country to sell.

Independence, Independent - to be free of control, often meaning by another country, allowing the people of a nation the ability to govern themselves.

Industry - the part of the economy concerned with turning raw materials into into manufactured goods, for example making furniture from wood.

Intercontinental ballistic missile - a guided ballistic missile with a minimum range of 5,500km or 3,400 miles.

International relations - the relationships between different countries.

Iron Curtain - a phrase used by Winston Churchill to describe the non-physical divide created by Stalin between Eastern Europe and the West.

L

Legitimacy, Legitimate - accepted by law or conforming to the rules; can be defended as valid.

Liberal - politically, someone who believes in allowing personal freedom without too much control by the government or state.

M

Military force - the use of armed forces.

Minister - a senior member of government, usually responsible for a particular area such as education or finance.

Monarchists - people in favour of living in a country governed by a monarchy.

N

Nationalism, Nationalist, Nationalistic - identifying with your own nation and supporting its interests, often to the detriment or exclusion of other nations.

P

Poverty - the state of being extremely poor.

Predecessor - the person who came before; the previous person to fill a role or position.

President - the elected head of state of a republic.

Propaganda - biased information aimed at persuading people to think a certain way.

Prosecute - to institute or conduct legal proceedings against a person or organisation.

Proxy war - a conflict between two sides acting on behalf of other parties who are not directly involved, but who have usually supplied equipment, arms and/or money.

Q

Quarantine - a period of isolation where a person or animal who has or may have a communicable disease is kept away from others.

R

Rebellion - armed resistance against a government or leader, or resistance to other authority or control.

Reform, Reforming - change, usually in order to improve an institution or practice.

Refugee, Refugees - a person who has been forced to leave where they live due to war, disaster or persecution.

Reparations - payments made by the defeated countries in a war to the victors to help pay for the cost of and damage from the fighting.

Repressive - a harsh or authoritarian action; usually used to describe governmental abuse of power.

Republic - a state or country run by elected representatives and an elected/nominated president. There is no monarch.

Revolution - the forced overthrow of a government or social system by its own people.

Rig, Rigged - politically, to interfere in or fix an election to determine the winner.

S

Sanctions - actions taken against states who break international laws, such as a refusal to trade with them or supply necessary commodities.

Satellite state - a country under the control of another, such as countries under USSR control during the Cold War.

Segregation - when people are kept separately from each other - often used in the context of race.

Sino - is a a reference to China or something relating to China. It is a prefix which is used instead of China.

Socialism - a political and economic system where most resources, such as factories and businesses, are owned by the state or workers with the aim of achieving greater equality between rich and poor.

Soviet - an elected workers' council at local, regional or national level in the former Soviet Union. It can also be a reference to the Soviet Union or the USSR.

Sphere of influence - an area or country under the influence of another country.

Stalemate - a situation where no action can be taken and neither side can make progress against the other; effectively a draw.

Standard of living - level of wealth and goods available to an individual or group.

State, States - an area of land or a territory ruled by one government.

T

Tactic - a strategy or method of achieving a goal.

Territories, Territory - an area of land under the control of a ruler/country.

Thaw - the period of time where the relationship between the USSR and the USA improved.

Treaty - a formal agreement, signed and ratified by two or more parties.

Tsar - the Russian word for emperor; can also be spelled 'czar'.

V

Veto - the right to reject a decision or proposal.

W

Western powers - a group term used to describe developed capitalist nations, such as Britain and the USA.

Quizzes, amazing exam preparation tools and more at GCSEHistory.com

Milton Keynes UK
Ingram Content Group UK Ltd.
UKHW050351081023
430100UK00006B/37